THE BEAT GOES ON

LYNN REGUDON

authorHOUSE®

AuthorHouse™
1663 Liberty Drive
Bloomington, IN 47403
www.authorhouse.com
Phone: 1 (800) 839-8640

Published by AuthorHouse 07/18/2016

ISBN: 978-1-5246-1865-0 (sc)
ISBN: 978-1-5246-1863-6 (hc)
ISBN: 978-1-5246-1864-3 (e)

Library of Congress Control Number: 2016911323

PROLOGUE

When I first began working at King County Hospital in the 1950s (now known as Harborview Medical Center), the hospital served the welfare and indigent population of Seattle and King County in the days before Medicare and Medicaid. Those who could pay were sent to private institutions as soon as they were stable. The hospital operated under the aegis of the county government until the University of Washington Medical School took it over, by which time I was gone. Across our paychecks there was always a stamp that said "From funds not otherwise appropriated." Sometimes those funds had been otherwise appropriated, I was told, and paychecks had to be held a few days to a week until there was money in the county coffers to cash them. It never happened while I was there, but that gives a clue to the facilities. To call the surroundings "minimalist" would be kind. Windows had no screens. Air conditioning was a faraway dream. The original Emergency Room had a narrow alley-like entrance allowing only one car or ambulance through at a time, with room for a maximum of two vehicles to park. Electric typewriters were just beginning to come in, and IBM's innovative Selectric did not make it to market until about 1963, two years after I left. Bill Gates was only a baby.

In the decade after World War II, we had more than our share of drunks, but we did not have the enormous drug problems emergency rooms face now. The human problems, however, were not markedly different. We saw our share of tragedies and had our moments of utter silliness or annoyance at patients, doctors, and other staff.

As psychologists have long noted, memories are imperfect, swayed by a myriad of influences. If you ask your grown children what they remember about the vacation you took when they were ten, what they say may make you wonder if you were on the same trip. So I do not claim even the participants will remember events exactly the way I have--if they remember them at all. Conversations included, of course, are not the exact words, but meant to capture the spirit of the event. While I have used the real name of the hospital, the names of patients, most of the staff, and all those from outside services, such as police and ambulance personnel have been changed to maintain confidentiality. To be sure, some may recognize themselves or others if they were present during the same episodes—or they may not. At the time of this writing, many of those I worked with are dead; I may not have changed their names. The names of home town friends and my family are real, as are some staff members.

The stories in this book are about the people I met at King County Hospital. These are vignettes of staff, patients, and doctors, caught in a particular time and place. The reader will be introduced to some of the other players in the hospital milieu, and behind-the-scene activities, never (or rarely) mentioned by nurse/physician authors. Admittedly, I have left out many people I worked with, as well as whole departments, such as Social Services, primarily because my interactions with these people were spotty, and/or short-lived. Most of the last have died.

Here is a glimpse into the world of medicine, circa the 1950s, before many of the amazing machines that now make up the hospital's routine, when nurses still wore white uniforms, caps, and pins that distinguished the schools where they trained, and to the place that took me from a somewhat shy, naive geography student to a more seasoned young woman, starting me on the path to my final job in healthcare information management.

PILGRIMAGE

Today is Sunday. No parking meters to feed. This June afternoon in Seattle is warm and sunny, a perfect time to visit Harborview Medical Center, where my life changed forever.

Only decorative now, a new glass-domed canopy protects the visitor from Seattle's ubiquitous rain. The entry steps are the same, perhaps a little more worn. The great metal doors still open as easily. The marble-floored lobby, now covered with an undistinguished gray rug, is as unwelcoming as it was when I first entered some sixty-plus years ago to interview for a job. The old telephone operator's window is boarded up, and a computer sits on a desk in front of it, unmanned.

Do not tarry, the room whispers; but I do, remembering. Up the few steps to the first floor hallway, my hand rests for a moment on the decorative iron hand rail before crossing to push the down button on the elevator. The next floor below is "ground," just as it was, and I press it.

Exiting the elevator, I turn right, as I did then, but now nothing is familiar. The wide hallway's silvery floor shines brightly; gone are the dull red-and-black rubber tiles of my day. The signs over the new doors are totally different: Radiology, Gamma Knife, Angiography. There are no benches for patients as there were. I am relieved I am alone to walk toward what used to be the Medical Records Department. Double doors now demarcate the end of the original building, opening into another corridor in the first of the new wings to be added. Turning around, I head back down the corridor toward where the Emergency Department and the cafeteria once were. Neither is there. A sign announces that the cafeteria is on B level, and a long corridor at a right angle to the one I am in points to the "West Hospital." I follow this hall, which skirts a huge glass dome. I am guessing it is where the old ambulance court was for the original emergency room. Now it provides natural light for the cafeteria below.

Back up on the first floor, I follow the sign pointing to the Emergency Department, now on the north side of the building. Through the door there is a bank of stations, a chair in front of each. A young man in white sits behind the first, marked "Triage." No patients are sitting at his station or the two other manned stations.

How different from the one office for the admitting clerk, when I worked there. This Sunday there are only a few people scattered in the expansive, thriftily furnished waiting room. No one looks stressed. I wonder how different it will be on the evening and night shifts.

Back to the elevator, I push the button for B level. Strangely, down here, there are remnants I recognize: masses of pipes running along the ceiling, doors opening to corridors that pass under the street that don't look as if they had been replaced since I worked there. Some men in gray coveralls pass by with tools in their hands. I smile to myself. Perhaps some things don't change as quickly.

Down the corridor that says "Cafeteria" in search of a cup of coffee, I find it modern and up-to-date with an espresso stand. Small tables are spread about the large room under the skylight, and more, farther away in its murky reaches. With coffee in hand, I find a seat under the glass dome and put my camera down. I observe the clientele sprinkled about: a man in a white coat, graying at the temples, with a well-dressed young black woman; a younger man in a lab coat concentrating on a laptop computer; two women in surgical greens giggling over sandwiches and coffee; several lone men and women, more disheveled, secreted in the darker corners of the cafeteria. I remove the lens cap from my camera and take a few pictures as unobtrusively as possible.

Finishing my coffee, I make my way out back of the hospital where a landscaped garden creates a quiet haven of lush green lawn amid raised flower beds with concrete surrounds where one can sit, savoring the vista of Seattle and its harbor with a sparkling Puget Sound and the snow-capped Olympic Mountains in the background. A young woman in blue scrubs sits reading on one of the benches scattered around the periphery. A bare-chested, black-haired man in his early thirties wearing threadbare Levi's leans against one of the concrete-rimmed flower beds, a colored shirt drying in the sun draped over a bush nearby. In another corner of the lawn are two wooden raised beds, one short, the one behind it taller. It bears a plaque that says, "This garden was developed for and is maintained by HMC patients during rehabilitation therapy. Please enjoy but do not pick the flowers. Thank you." That definitely warrants a photograph.

I replace the lens cap and make my way back to the car. So many changes in the years since I worked there.

Thinking back, I realize the cascade of events that led me here started with a casual conversation between me and a housemate in my hometown of Hamilton, New York. I was seventeen, a senior in high school.

My mother had married her third husband the summer before and moved to a nearby town. To let me finish in the school where I had begun my education, she rented our house to the mother of a classmate at a reduced rate with the proviso that I could stay there. Mrs. Lanigan; her daughter and my classmate, Mary Alice; Mrs. L's two older sons, Chuck and John; and Wally, one of their close friends made up the household. All three boys were students at Colgate University in town, and it was Wally who became my best buddy that year.

One winter night, nursing hot toddies for snuffly noses, Wally had been telling me about his family and asked, "What about your dad? Do you hear from him very often?"

"I've never heard from him. Don't even know if he's still alive. Mom never talked about him."

"Don't you know anything about him? No pictures even?"

"Not really. The only pictures I've seen were ones of him standing on his hands on top of a cannon, and on top of my grandparents' home up on the hill. He graduated from Colgate, too; that's where Mom met him."

"Aren't you curious about him?"

Wally's comment spurred me to write my paternal grandfather, who lived in Redlands, California, where I was born. He sent me a birthday card every year so I had his address. I enclosed a rather diffident letter to forward to that unknown father if he were still alive. Within the month, I received an *epistle*—many pages, in small, elegant handwriting, from that long-lost man. He erased in the first sentence any question about whether he cared. He proposed I come to live with his family and attend the University of Washington, where he taught English. He laid out a plan and introduced my new family. I had applied and been accepted at Duke, Bowling Green in

Ohio, and Redlands universities, but had not decided. Here was the answer, and there was no question in my mind. My mother was not pleased, but gave in.

Stepping off the plane in Seattle, I was greeted with a warm hug from the dapper, distinguished-looking man, graying at the temples, who was my father. I fell in love immediately. A hug from his wife, Flossie, and smiles, partly curious, from my new-found half-brothers, Glen, Jr. and Trevor. My new family—the adventure had begun.

Fall came, and I registered at the university, one of my first classes being a survey of architecture. High in the gallery of an auditorium holding two hundred, I sat next to an Indian student with a great mop of black hair and gorgeous long-lashed brown eyes, who introduced himself as Nazir Jairazbhoy. We met again off and on at the International Club, which my father had suggested I join. Over the next year we dated often, and he asked me to marry him—often. At first I refused, but he wore me down and in February of 1949, we made it official at the County Clerk's office, accompanied by my family.

Born in India, the son of a British teacher, my father liked Nazir, but my stepmother informed me quietly that marriage was not as acceptable—an old attitude pervasive among the Colonial British that Indians were "inferior." However, Dad kept his own council and did not voice his disapproval to my husband or me.

Nazir and I found out quickly that two cannot live as cheaply as one, and his allowance from India did not go very far. By fall of 1950, it became obvious one of us had to work. He obtained a summer job at Bethlehem Steel until they discovered he was on a student visa, which did not allow him to work in the United States, so he had to quit. (His job title there was priceless—Helper to the Helper of the Punch Press.) Having only enough money to register Nazir for fall classes, I started looking for work. The employment agency sent me to interview at King County Hospital.

IN THE BEGINNING

Getting off the bus at Ninth and James, referral slip in hand, I could not miss the place where I had been sent for a job interview. King County Hospital rose before me, its fifteen stories soaring into the autumn sun, dwarfing the nearby buildings. I stood staring for a moment, feeling quite provincial. The little college town from which I had come had no buildings taller than five stories. The hospital stood like a sentinel guarding the top of First Hill, broad-shouldered, protective.

Wide steps and heavy metal-framed doors opened into a bare, marble-floored lobby. No comfortable chairs and tables with popular magazines here, no fish tanks to engage those who waited. No amenities at all. "Go about your business," was the implication.

The only sign of life was a little room with a Dutch door, opening on the right side of the lobby where two women manned a switchboard. Getting directions from one of them, I found my way to the Medical Records Department on the ground level at the end of a long, dimly lit hall. The woman behind the appointment desk motioned me into an alcove of offices on the other side of a large rectangular room. My memory of that first view of the department was the four-drawer steel cabinets lining the room almost all the way around. Files were piled on top of the cabinets, on big tables down the center of the room, and on top of desks. I had never seen so much paper. How did anyone find anything?

The assistant supervisor called my name, a bit hesitantly. "Roslyn...?" I smiled, used to the hesitation; my married name, Jairazbhoy, gave most people pause. At the end of the short interview, she announced that I had the job of file clerk, and could I start on Monday?

I went home, jubilant. My first full-time job! An end to searching bus stops for dimes and nickels, even pennies. I could hardly wait for Monday.

The first week on any new job is exhausting: new procedures to learn, names to remember, finding one's way around. Hospitals are like little cities. Sometimes it seems as though the architect has taken a perverse pleasure in devising interior corridors as labyrinthine as any Middle Eastern bazaar. It is so easy to get lost if you are new, but at least I could find my way to the department where I was to start working.

Entering the building down a ramp closest to the Medical Records Department on my first day, I was struck by the hallway: dingy, dark yellow walls, lined on one side by wooden chairs and what looked like old church pews. Patients filled these at this early hour, some disheveled, most wearing worn coats, and shoes run over on the sides or heels. "Tatterdees" my father would have called them. Children of sick parents ran up and down the hallway. Sick children sat lethargically on adult laps. At the appointment desk of the Medical Records Department, a short line of walk-in patients waited to have their names taken and be sent off to the appropriate department.

The diminutive, gray-haired department head, Miss Kellogg, a registered record librarian, as the practitioners were then known, gave me a brief orientation to the department. She had me sign the necessary forms, explained my hours and the very few fringe benefits. She told me to buy a white uniform as soon as possible, and gave me my first assignment.

"We'll have you start on the appointment desk," she said. "Mary and Stella will give you a good introduction to the basic procedures. Don't be afraid to ask questions if you don't understand something or can't find a chart."

The appointment desk, enclosed by wood partitions on two sides and a partial glass window facing the hall, was just big enough to accommodate two people sitting. I found out quickly, usually only Mary sat. On the desk were six pads, each a different color. One was for the Emergency Room (ER), and the rest were for the different clinics scheduled that day. Not only did Mary have to deal with the constant flow of patients at the window, but she also had to answer the phone for chart requests from the clinics and the ER. She was a wonder of calm. With the phone ringing, she could still smile at the patient at the window and ask the person on the phone to "Please hold just a minute," while writing on a pad, or giving the patient a card with the clinic name and appointment date. (I wondered in passing why they hadn't found something for her to do with her feet at the same time.)

The clinics usually had the patient's medical record number, which was how the records were filed. The ER requests most often had only the patient's name and birthdate, by which to find the record number in the master patient index. For the first few days, I was given only the chart requests that already had numbers, and did not have to check patients' names against the index. I had enough to learn just to find charts.

Stella, a tall thin young woman, a few years older than my just-barely-twenty explained the filing system. I followed her around like a puppy dog the first day, while she kept up a constant discourse on where the charts most likely would be found. Despite the ring of cabinets lining the entire department, they held only six months' worth of charts. When a patient hadn't been seen in that time, the chart was sent back to inactive storage, a city block down the hall, or so it seemed.

The storage room most closely resembled library stacks. Lights hung between the rows from the high ceiling, casting more shadow than illumination on the sturdy wooden shelves. These were about ten tiers high, with rolling ladders attached to each section and a few portable ones at aisle ends. The woman in charge of inactive storage was Harriet, maybe 50 years old, thin, with gray hair pulled back into a bun. She was not particularly communicative, and while pleasant enough on the phone, she was decidedly not excited about new employees. She looked at me with obvious misgivings.

"I hope you're more careful with the records than most of the new ones," she said, looking over the top of her bifocals at me "You must understand that a misfiled chart means there is no information about that patient for the doctors. That could be a lot of trouble for the patient. See to it you don't file anything here that I don't check. Understand?"

I smiled and nodded, and silently determined I would not be an example of "those new ones."

By the end of the week, I had learned where to find most charts and get them to their scheduled destination, as well as most of the places charts could hide when they weren't in the regular files.

Late one afternoon toward the middle of the week, I decided to check one for ER with only a name and birthdate, John Johnson. "Have you used the master patient index before?" Mary asked me.

"No," I replied and thought, *how hard can that be? I know how to alphabetize.*

As I went over to the index files, I heard Mary tell Stella, "You'd better help her. I don't think she's looked anything up yet."

Slightly miffed, I confidently went to the J's and discovered to my consternation that the names starting with J were in no alphabetic order I could detect. Stella watched my confusion and chuckled. Then she pointed to an instruction sheet attached at each end of the bank of cabinets. This identified the method as Soundex, a phonetic system using the sound of consonants after the first letter of the last name to create a three-digit code, ignoring vowels. Johnson was found behind J-525, the codable letters n-s-n, then filed alphabetically by first name. There were John Johnsons, Jensens, Jansens, Johansens and more behind this J-525 code. At last I found the John Johnson with the right birthdate. There must have been 500 Johns. Well, perhaps I exaggerate. Soundex proved so interesting that I took the instructions home and practiced on the phone book. By the beginning of the next week, I was an expert.

With that mastered, Stella introduced me to registering new patients. This involved filling out a "stat" (statistics) card with the required information, typing the basic demographic data onto a new patient registration sheet, then making a plate with the name and new hospital number. The machine used to imprint the metal plate made a thunderous racket. The plate was used like early credit cards, run through a machine that imprinted paper so handwriting was unnecessary. Aside from typewriters, that was about as high tech as the Medical Records Department got in the 1950s, in a hospital whose money came from "funds not otherwise appropriated."

Each night those first weeks, I flopped like a rag doll into the car when Nazir came to pick me up. My head swam with all the new procedures, finding all the places I was sent, and trying to remember the names of all the new people I had met. But it was a good type of fatigue. I was pleased with my progress there and how much I had picked up. I liked the people I worked with, and looked forward to my job.

By the end of the next couple of months, I had mastered the procedures for my job, and was eager to learn something new. I could now relieve at the appointment desk, although I never was as sanguine as Mary under the pressure of phone and patients. I could find most misplaced charts, and could follow the path of a record from its removal from the file to its return, whatever circuitous route it took. Sometimes a bit of detective work was required, and the challenge was satisfying. I filed records in the main office, but not in Harriet's domain, which suited me; the storage room was dark and dreary.

By now, I knew the registration process inside and out and I enjoyed the brief patient contacts. I led the new patient into the glassed-in registration booth next to the appointment desk and my first question was if he or she had ever been a patient there before. I might get a quick "no," or sometimes a pause and "I'm not sure." If the latter answer was from a woman, the next question was whether there were other last names she might have used. I asked people to spell their last names, no matter how simple; variations were common. The tricky question was birthdate. One elderly woman gave the month and day, but when I prompted her for the year, she said, "I'm 82. You figure it out." Sometimes the older patients couldn't remember their age, and the relative with them didn't know either, at which point I usually asked for the patient's best guess, and we went from there. The usual demographic data like address, birth place, occupation, nearest relative, and parents' names were less of a problem, though relatives often did not know the latter.

Communicating with those whose English was limited proved a challenge, but I picked up on accents fairly quickly. Stella taught me to ask those born in China for their "family name" rather than last name, because the order is different from English.

With registration procedures under my belt, Mrs. Nelson, the assistant supervisor, sent me over to Emergency for training in the admitting office.

At that time, admitting clerks were employees of the Medical Record Department, because they needed to know the same procedures necessary to register patients and find charts. Unlike Medical Records, which closed about 10 PM, ER admitting was staffed around the clock.

I had been in the ER many times to bring them records, but now I paid new attention to my surroundings. The ambulance entrance was the focal point. A spiked iron fence blocked the ambulances or cars from hitting the skylights that illuminated part of the basement. A big, wide door, surprisingly easy to open for its size, led into the ER, with the nursing station on the left, a large treatment room on the right of the entrance, and two more behind that.

The admitting office was just behind the nurses' station down the hall. Behind that was a longer room with four beds, euphemistically called the observation ward. The elevator at the end of the hallway was strictly for patients being admitted or taken to X-ray.

In my new bailiwick, a tall, rarely-washed window looked out over the ambulance court. Charts of discharged ER patients sat in a basket on the ledge, waiting to be returned to Medical Records Department. At a worn wooden desk with a black laminate top Julia, the day admitting clerk and my new mentor, sat in a swivel chair, typing on an electric typewriter (joy!) with an accounting carriage, probably recycled from the Business Office. She motioned me to sit in the single cane-backed chair in front of the desk. For reasons unclear to me, a wash basin hung precariously from the wall just inside the door.[1]

Putting a completed stat card in a basket in front of the typewriter, Julia explained my duties in detail, and showed me where to find lists and supplies that I would need.

Then a nurse popped around the corner. "Julia, the patient in one is going to Ortho—fractured femur."

"Well, here you go, Lynn," Julia said, handing me an empty clipboard. She took the stat card from the ER chart, and handed it to me. "The patients don't come to you usually. You go to them."

I took the clipboard and began my new duties. I saw patients in the ER hallway, in a treatment room, or outside the admitting office on a stretcher on the way to the elevator. Sometimes, depending on the patient's condition, I obtained my data from someone accompanying him, who might not have all the information I needed. Patients were not always happy about being questioned. On new patients, one item I had to get was their mother's maiden name. That frequently elicited a "what d'ya need that for?" It was necessary to fill out the death certificate, I had been told; somehow that didn't seem like the most tactful answer. "The state requires it," was my stock response.

Toward the end of the shift, Julia got up from behind the desk and plopped a couple of discharged charts in front of me. "These two were brought in by Seattle police, and you have to report any like that to Complaints. One of those is a traffic accident. The numbers you need to call for reporting are here." She pointed to a sheet on the wall. "We do it at the end of shift, but if you can't get to it, leave it for the next shift."

Just as the evening clerk arrived and Julia was preparing to leave, she turned and said, "I almost forgot. If anyone is actually sent back to pay their bill, we charge three dollars for a routine ER visit, and five dollars if they had sutures. It almost never happens, but in the bottom drawer there's a cash box with twenty dollars in it. We take it up to the Business Office in the morning if anyone has paid." (Given the cost of an ER visit today, these prices seem ludicrous, but no one even batted an eyelash in 1950.)

By the end of the week, I had learned the routines and a few things about myself. Having to interview patients who were vomiting elicited a sympathetic reaction in my own gut. Swallowing after asking each question kept me from being as big a problem as they were. Seeing bloody and severely injured patients oddly did not trouble me, and I could maintain a poker face while talking to them.

As I began to relieve more frequently in admitting, I found that occasionally a patient's condition was too serious to allow time to get the required information, although the nurse always obtained the patient's name, address, and birthdate when he arrived, so at least we had the basics. Sometimes I followed the patient to the floor, or went later in the shift to see if I could complete the data. Once I went with the orderly and a fourth year medical student to the OR where the patient was to be prepped for immediate surgery. The medical student was trying to catheterize him with little success. Standing at the foot of the stretcher, I stopped talking each time the patient flinched. Finally the resident said, "Keep asking your questions, and distract him." I moved to the head of the stretcher and kept him talking until they were successful.

I understood patients in pain might get angry with me for asking questions and did not take it personally. Drunks, however, could be pretty abusive at times. One fairly articulate but intoxicated patient had refused to give anything but his name to anyone, nurses, and doctors alike. The nurse brought me the stat card and said, "Good luck. Be careful; he's really belligerent." I found him in the back hallway on a stretcher and after much cussing he gave me his address. I noticed, in passing, that he had a pin on his lapel that indicated the Independent Order of Foresters. "Are you a Forester?" I asked.

"Yes," he replied. "So?"

"So am I." I really was a member of that fraternal group. My statement turned him into a smiling pussycat. I was now an ally and easily completed my data quest. One never knew what would turn someone around.

But the psych patients could be scary and you could never predict what would turn them around, either. One afternoon, the orderly brought a patient by the office, well strapped down on a gurney, and said, "Better not talk to this one." I persisted, however—determined to get that information as there was no relative with her. Already having the basics, I asked her religious preference. She looked at me hard—wild-eyed—then burst out of the straps, jumped off the gurney, and ran down the hall. The orderly and a nurse, along with a passing resident, tore after her. They finally got her wrestled back down on the stretcher and into the elevator to the fifth floor, the psychiatric ward. The orderly had a few strong words for me when he came back. I learned if I was told not to ask, I didn't, and got my information some other way.

At the end of five months I could relieve in admitting and even take an entire day shift by myself. By the sixth month, I was assigned as a float, to relieve in Admitting on all three shifts.

The greatest challenge in the ER—and most interesting—was the occasional John or Jane Doe. These patients required a little detective work which added spice to the routine.

During the wee hours one morning, a man was brought in by ambulance. Assaulted in a waterfront bar, all his money was gone but the thieves kindly left his wallet. He was passed-out drunk and snoring away, but with a possible head injury. The orderly and I went through all his pockets and the wallet, finding a card which identified him as Hjalmer Johansen and gave his address as a post office box in Ketchikan, Alaska. It also identified him as a member of a seaman's union. A driver's license issued in Washington gave his birthdate, but only a PO box address in Westport, a fishing village on the Washington coast. There was no Hjalmer Johansen in the telephone directory, and far too many Johansens to justify a call in the middle of the night. On another torn sheet of paper was a name, James Curtis, address of Seattle, no street, and the prefix only of a phone number, which at that time was in letters (e.g. WE, AT, LA) correlating with the area of town. The name, James Curtis, was less common than John Smith, but there were still many in the phone book, and more than one with the same telephone prefix

We had enough data to determine the man was a new patient, but we would have to wait until later in the morning to contact the seaman's union, and try to find more information. Perhaps by then the man would have slept off his inebriated state and be alert enough to give some answers without having to disturb strangers. I held on to the stat card, making notes about the union card and name he had written down, along with a list of possibles from the telephone book and left it for the next shift. Out of curiosity, I followed up when I came to work the next night. The day shift clerk had called the union hall, obtained a little more information, and had called several of the numbers I had left before finding a James Curtis who said he was acquainted with the patient, but knew of no relatives. Unfortunately, as it turned out, the man never regained consciousness, and he died of his head injury. However, some weeks later, a relative of the patient called and threatened a lawsuit because he had not been notified. Given the circumstances, and because we had made a good faith effort, the case never came to trial. A terse memo from the hospital administrator let it be known to all of us in the ER how important it was to get all current and accurate information.

Getting ordinary patient information might seem a straightforward task, and this was true most of the time. You've probably had to answer such questions at least once in a hospital setting. But how good would your memory be when you were in pain with a broken arm, or having difficulty breathing? Would you even remember your address? Or would you be able to communicate this information in a foreign country where you didn't understand the language very well—if at all? If a relative brought you in, could he answer questions for you? Can your spouse remember your birthday--the *year* you were born (if you were honest about that to begin with), or your mother's maiden name? If you were having a heart attack, I'll bet you, too, would have said, "What d'ya need that for?" How about the name and address of your nearest relative, if not a spouse? What kind of work you do? You see? It isn't always easy to get good information even under reasonable circumstances.

When we found several patients with the same name and same birth month and day, we compared addresses, birth years, spouses' names. If none of those parameters matched, we were usually safe in assigning a new number. Psychiatric patients could be most creative. We had some who used totally different names, first, last, or both, depending on their mood. One of our regular psychiatric patients had to be cross-referenced on a regular basis: she had used at least ten different names. Fortunately, the nursing staff on all shifts knew her so well they could give us alternatives if the one she gave wasn't on file. Curiously, many gave their real birthdates for all their aliases.

Sometimes the person was reluctant to give his or her name for less obvious reasons—fear of being arrested, fear of having relatives notified, a personal desire for anonymity, or for reasons we never learned.

But the bulk of our John and Jane Doe patients were because of injury or illness, not reticence. (And yes, there were a few whose real names were John or Jane Doe.) Difficulty understanding speech due to injury, strokes or language barriers also made for problems. The patients we had the hardest time identifying were those who had been assaulted and were unconscious. They usually had no identification and we could only go by the little information the police gave us, if any at all.

We had some options. If the patient had any identification, we could go through everything he had—always with two people present. This was our starting point. Name and birthdate were easy if there was a driver's license. The address might or might not be correct, but it was a starting point. Finding a relative or friend to contact was more of a challenge. Sometimes there was a card identifying an employer; we called when possible.

One night a patient was brought back to me with a name and address only. A silent, expansive mound on the gurney, a small line of drool ran out of one side of his mouth, which drooped a little lower on that side. He had been found by a neighbor who, unable to get a response, called the ambulance. He was conscious but obviously had had a stroke. The diagnosis on the stat card read "CVA with expressive aphasia" (cerebrovascular accident with inability to speak coherently). He was middle-aged, quite overweight, and the neighbor had found him sitting in the lotus position. The doctor thought his crossed legs, combined with his obesity, must have loosened a blood clot, probably from a deep vein thrombosis, which then became an embolus to the brain. I glanced at him to see if maybe I could get a yes or no response, and was startled to recognize him as a close friend of a picture framer I knew. The two were heavily into Scientology and Asian mysticism, explaining the attempted lotus position. Realizing I could get nothing from the patient, I went back to the office and called the framer despite the early morning hour. I was able to get additional information and a promise for follow-up in the morning when he would go to the patient's apartment and check for a possible relative's name and address. This event turned out much better than the seaman who died: the patient survived and returned home with advice to lose some weight before trying yoga positions again.

Although situations like the above were infrequent, digging for whatever information could be found and putting the disparate pieces together made my job immensely satisfying.

TO INDIA - HIATUS AND RETURN

"Miss Kellogg, I'm afraid I have to give my notice." I sat in her office after only seven months on the job. "My husband's visa expires next month and he has to return to India, so we'll be leaving in early June. I want to say how much I've enjoyed working here."

She smiled. "We're sorry to lose you, but it sounds quite exciting. Please do drop us a line and let us know how you're doing."

Two weeks later, the beginning of June, 1951, my husband and I left Seattle for the long trip that ultimately landed us in India. How can I summarize in a few paragraphs the experiences of the ten months we were in Bombay, before we again returned to the United States?

I'd never traveled outside my own country, and the prospect of living abroad was both exciting and unnerving. Nazir, already a seasoned world traveler when I first met him, made all the necessary arrangements. We sailed from New York to Southampton, my first voyage on a large ship. From his trust fund at Lloyd's Bank, we were able to do a bit of sightseeing in and around London before we returned to port to catch the P&O liner for the twenty-eight day trip to Bombay,.

In his own country, Nazir was a wealthy man and finding immediate work was not a priority. Getting acquainted with his family proved an easy task—they all spoke English and were very welcoming. I already knew his brother Amir and wife, Bibi (Shireen), from their own student days at the University of Washington, but meeting his half-brother, Ashraf, the family solicitor, and his wife, Zareen, and other members was delightful. The wives were very helpful in acclimating me to the customs and helping me shop. After so many years of only window-shopping, it seemed strange to actually be able to buy! They tried to teach me how to bargain, but I was never good at it. The ladies also taught me how to wrap a sari, and later, how to deal with a tailor—both an art form. And, finally, Nazir bought me a wedding ring, which we designed together and had made. I learned that in India you never left a piece of jewelry with the jeweler—you stayed and watch the work being done.

The grinding poverty was evident everywhere we looked. Beggars were always at our heels. "Pay no attention to them," Nazir advised me, but it was hard to do. Being in American dress, I was a "foreigner" and clearly better game than the natives. If I walked alone, I was besieged; less so when I was with friends or family. I learned to respond with, *"Nehi, nehi, jaldi jao!"* (No, no, go away quickly.)

Offsetting this, though, were the young entrepreneurs, who offered to "watch your car" and/or clean it. These boys would ask a few *pice* for this service and a little more to clean it. "It's a good idea to let them do that," Nazir told me. "If you don't, you might find things missing when you come back." There were no dirty cars in Bombay.

We got to know a couple of boys near Ashraf's office where we went often. The boys were about ten and fourteen, I guessed. They were bright kids and friendly; we taught them new English words each time we parked, and they eagerly displayed their good memories the next time we came.

Ashraf had arranged our lodging at a hotel on Marine Drive, overlooking Back Bay, until we could find a place of our own. Nazir took me to see their original family home, Gulshan, found on top of a hill overlooking the Arabian Sea, at the end of Jairazbhoy Lane (imagine—a street named after one's own family!). The grounds were lush with well-tended tropical flowers and palms and a green lawn, complete with a peacock and a cobra--the latter with which we fortunately made no acquaintance. At that time it was being used as a college, which tells you something about the size of his boyhood home.

Nazir quickly tired of having to use Ashraf's car and driver to get around, so he purchased a car. Our travels expanded exponentially, usually with friends on weekends, as most had to work during the week.

One of the most lingering memories of India I have was on our final night in Aurangabad, our base for a tour of the nearby Ellora and Ajanta caves carved into the cliffside. We also went to see the *Bibi ka Maqbara,* or *Chota* [little] Taj, built by Aurangzeb's son, Azam, to commemorate his mother's death, a smaller version of the Taj Mahal. We went at midnight, and it was magical. The night was clear, stars filled an indigo sky. Standing close to the wrought-iron gates, the monument's white marble gleamed in the moonlight. We stood holding hands, completely enamored of the beauty before us. It was hard to come back to Earth that night.

On our return to Bombay, Nazir decided we had to find a real place to live. After many considerations, he found a flat on the top floor of a new building. Then began my real induction into Indian culture. Having done paid housework as a teenager, I now found myself in charge of servants. This was serious culture shock. I had a cook, a tailor, a dhobi (laundryman), a man to clean the flat, another to clean the bathroom, all of whom lived elsewhere. And I had to speak with them in Urdu, which I hardly knew except for a few phrases. I learned, too, that I could not treat them in the same egalitarian way I had been treated.

"They won't respect you, and will rob you blind," Bibi admonished me.

We settled in to ordinary life. Nazir spent most days away from the flat with friends of his architect brother, and evenings, they often spent with us. Gradually, Nazir came to the conclusion that he needed to return to the University of Washington to get his degree in architecture. I was not happy about that. I enjoyed the family and friends we had, and I didn't want to return. But Nazir was adamant, and he made the arrangements for our return to coincide with Ashraf and Zareen's trip through Europe.

It was on the leg of our travels in Italy that I became very nauseated and unable to eat. (In Italy? Travesty!) Zareen was to see a doctor in Switzerland about some of her own health issues, and arranged for me to see him, too. He told me I was pregnant. Nazir seemed somewhat ambivalent about the news, which made me uneasy.

Finally, one year and one day since our original departure, we again entered the United States, Nazir with a resident alien visa, and I, pregnant.

Our baby girl, Nish, was born in January, 1953, and Nazir's reason for returning to the United States was put on hold. He took a couple of jobs he hated and soon quit, leaving us in the same financial situation we had been in as students. Then he started painting with the expectation of selling enough pictures to make a living, but art work was hard to sell.

So about September of 1953, I called Miss Kellogg at the hospital to find out whether there were any openings. As luck would have it, there was one. She was happy to have someone fill the job who did not need training.

BACK IN THE SADDLE

On my first day back, there were changes that could not be ignored. Construction of a new wing had begun, leaving the south wall of the Medical Records Department (MRD) exposed outside but still intact. Earth movers were busy; jack hammers' ear-splitting rat-a-tat-tat as they broke up concrete; workers shouted to each other. Inside the department, the racket was deafening. The appointment desk clerk had to shout to patients at the window who could barely hear her. One hundred feet down the hall, however, her words came through loud and clear. Fortunately, most of the work in the MRD required little conversation to get done.

The cast of characters had changed somewhat. Mary was gone from the appointment desk and Stella had left. My bosses were still there, as was Harriet in the inactive storage room. One of the file clerks new to me was Tomiko, a tiny Japanese woman. I went to lunch with her one of my first days back.

I asked whether she had been in one of the detention camps during the war.

"No, we were in Japan," she replied. "We went to visit family, but the war broke out, and we weren't allowed to leave. We were in Hiroshima."

At my "Oh my God!" she told me the rest of her story.

The day the atom bomb was dropped, Tomiko was in Tokyo. If my memory is correct, she said her family lived far enough outside Hiroshima so the bomb did not have the disastrous effects on them that it had on other residents closer in.

"In some ways, we were better off than our friends here," she told me. "We weren't surrounded by barbed wire fences. We had shortages of everything, and the fire bombings...." She paused and shivered. "But we could move around." I wondered what she wasn't saying and what they had lost here, but she said nothing more.

Tomiko was a hard worker and dogged. If a chart could not be found, the task was given to her. She never gave up until she located it, which often meant searching every nook and cranny in the entire clinic wing of the hospital. If a day went by and she couldn't find it, we assumed it had been swallowed up in the same kind of black hole that swallows socks in washing machines. Unlike socks, however, most charts eventually reappeared.

Other than tweaks in a few procedures, everything was familiar and within a few weeks I felt like I had never left. Because of the enormous back-log of unfiled lab reports, I was assigned to do "miscellaneous filing" at the beginning. This consisted of boxes of laboratory test results, each test recorded on a separate slip. The slips were small and tissue-paper thin. All had to be in numerical order. Each time a chart was pulled for a clinic, the boxes of lab work had to be checked and any found were attached to the backing sheet with scotch tape, hopefully in approximate date order. The back-log was measured in feet! All file clerks had to work on this job if they had any extra time. The haphazard procedure resulted in records that were often not adequately updated or accurate. It was also expensive, as lab work was frequently done again because the results weren't in the chart. As I recall, I spent most of that first week back on this nightmarish job and did whittle the boxes down a few inches. But oh, how I hated to see the lab people come down each night with a new batch. It was rather like shoveling snow in a blizzard.

Once Miss Kellogg was satisfied that I remembered the procedures, she again had me relieve in the admitting office, at first just for breaks during the day and then later for days off. I vividly remember the first evening shift I had to handle alone. Business was brisk and by 10 PM. I was running between the Medical Records Department, inactive storage way down the hall, and admitting—and I do mean running. Registering patients, finding charts, and getting others admitted made me frazzled. Then suddenly a muscle in one eyelid began to twitch. It became harder to see, and I'm sure I looked peculiar. By the time the night clerk came, however, the twitching had stopped and I was back to normal.

The construction/deconstruction and chaos going on at the hospital felt a bit like my marriage, which was also coming apart at the seams. Nish was now at a babysitter's all day, and once we picked her up and I made dinner, Nazir was gone, leaving me increasingly alone. The arguments escalated. Nish cried a lot, and often nothing I did consoled her. I was tired and felt like a bad mother. In my frustration and anger at my husband, I began to understand how child abuse occurred.

But the hospital was building something new, and for a time, I was determined to apply the analogy to my life as well. It was great to be back in a world I understood, and where I was treated like I had value.

Routines can be comforting. Getting back into the rhythm of familiar work and joining in the small talk with other employees felt good (when we could hear ourselves over the construction din).

With increasing conflict at home, work became a refuge. Getting to know a new batch of regulars among the patients made work even more interesting.

One of the more unusual clinic patients was a woman who had been the Fat Lady in a small town carnival. Following a heart attack in her early thirties, the doctor had recommended she find another occupation if she wanted to live to forty. At about five feet, three inches, she had been well over three hundred pounds, although when I first encountered her, she was already down to about two hundred pounds with the help of the clinic nutritionist. She was discouraged because it had been some time since she'd lost weight and I often saw her sitting in the waiting area looking depressed and tearful. But then one day several months later she came down from clinic all smiles.

"They're discharging me," she announced to Diane at the appointment desk. Holding her coat on one arm, she turned in a circle, displaying her now svelte one hundred forty-five pounds. We all clapped as she donned her now too-big coat and pushed open the old door to begin her new life.

"I think you're all wonderful," she said, "but I hope I never see you again." We retired the three volumes of her chart to storage.

ER, too, had its batch of regulars. There was Geneva, a skinny little southern lady in her mid-fifties born with congenital absence of forearms, with only a thumb on each of her foreshortened upper arms. She was diabetic but couldn't give herself the necessary daily insulin, so she came to the ER each morning. I often found her in the restroom, smoking a cigarette held between her vestigial thumb and arm. The nurses told me she was divorced, had a son, and sewed on an old treadle machine. I don't know if the last was true. I had a hard time picturing the "how" of that. She had a rather acid tongue and hated the cold, wet winters, as she had to travel to the hospital by bus. Her chart rarely left the ER except when she was seen in one of the clinics.

Mrs. Morgan was an asthmatic who got worse during the change of seasons. She was in her late fifties, slightly overweight, and would arrive wheezing loud enough to be heard down the hall. Once she got her shot, she sat in the waiting room for twenty minutes or so, the nurses checking on her to make sure she had no adverse reaction.

I didn't meet the Smith family until I started relieving on the evening shift. Especially during the winter, Loretta would arrive with all ten of her children, usually late in the evening. She was never happy about having to come in, but one or more of them always seemed to have an ear infection, or bronchitis, or some other minor problem.

"I can't never watch my TV shows at night," she complained. "There's always one of 'em who cries all the time and won't sleep, so I have to drag 'em all up here to get 'em fixed up."

Rumor had it none of the children had the same father, but who knew? Mom and the kids were thin and the little ones always seemed to have runny noses. They lived in Yesler Terrace just one block south of the hospital—convenient, considering the frequency with which they came in, or perhaps they came in so often because of the proximity. This was the era of Aid to Dependent Children, before welfare reform, and more kids meant more money, which meant even when the fathers took no responsibility, mothers could stay home with their children. Loretta, however, was on the extreme end of that continuum.

Among the regulars we got to know, too, were those who brought the patients. The drivers from the two major ambulance companies were well known to everyone in ER. The biggest company was

29

stationed in central Seattle close to Pill Hill, as First Hill was known because of the congregation of major hospitals there. The next largest ambulance company was in the southern part of the city. A few smaller companies serviced more outlying areas of the city and county. The drivers, unless told otherwise, always brought accident victims to King County Hospital, since it was considered the trauma hospital in the area, and was staffed 24-7 with physicians; the other hospitals were not. This guaranteed we saw the ambulance staffers regularly. The drivers and attendants were always good for some banter.

A special group of police were the warrant officers who brought patients destined to be evaluated for the weekly psychiatric hearings. These men had paperwork already, and simply gave it to us, bypassing the wait in ER and taking the patient directly to the fifth floor, psychiatry. Sometimes on the way back, they would stop and chat with whomever was at the nurses' station. They were a professional group of men, and we respected the fact their small talk never included stories about the patients they brought.

Seattle police were regular transporters of patients, sometimes people who were found on the street asking for help, or victims of muggings, fights or accidents. Sometimes the miscreants themselves were brought for evaluation or to have a wound sewed up and then be carted off to jail. Most often the officers were beat police, but sometimes we got detectives bringing in patients who were either suspected criminals or victims of a crime. The beat cops were pretty nice guys for the most part, but a few loud-mouths seemed to have joined the police force simply to be able to bully people legally. Nobody liked to see them coming. We kept those interchanges as short as possible. There was one ambulance driver who had trashed an African-American patient's apartment when he picked him up. He had been fired when the company found out, but then he managed to get into the police department and continued his ways as a prison guard—at least that's what one of the ambulance drivers told us. He was only marginally rehabilitated when he went through the police academy, after which we had the doubtful privilege of seeing him occasionally in the ER.

By early November, my own situation had deteriorated. One night Nazir took the last of our month's money and went up to Helen's Diner, where he used to win money playing the pinball machines before we were married. Despite having been told that no one paid out money for winning games any more, he was sure he could convince Helen to give him cash for games he won. She didn't. For me, it was the last straw.

My husband and I separated, he keeping our daughter since I didn't make enough money to pay a babysitter and he was living off his income from India, still not working. I told him I would come back if he got a job that actually paid money, but he did not, and it proved to be the end of a chapter. My stepmother told me, "You're going to regret leaving her with him." I knew she was right but didn't see any other options.

Nazir took Nish to be cared for by our best friends, Ruth and Gordon. For her first Christmas I made a little teal corduroy dress with fuzzy white piping. When I went to our friends' house to give it to her, Ruth had just put her to bed but brought her out. When Nish came over and put her tiny arms around my neck, I nearly lost it. I have carried the guilt of leaving her most of my life.

Unfortunately, Nazir paid for the divorce (his "last gallant act," he said) and left the country with Nish about a year later. I was devastated the day they left, but knew of no way to stop him. Indeed, the legal system at that time did not favor "mixed marriages." The judge in the family court, the only place I knew about that could have prevented him from leaving with Nish, had already made it clear in other decisions that any woman who married outside her ethnic background was not fit to be a parent.

From that time on, I threw myself into my job and returned to the university to finish my degree. My friends at work became my family.

THE HOSPITAL AND ITS PATIENTS

I confess I paid little attention to the patients at King County Hospital until I spent more time in the admitting office. Strange? Not when you consider my primary job in medical records dealt with paper— filing and pulling charts for clinics and running them around where needed. The professionals in the office then analyzed what was on that paper.

By the end of 1953 and early 1954, I'd started relieving in admitting on both evening and night shifts, covering for staff on their days off. There, I got a much better feel for the people whom we served. Ours was the only clinic and hospital where welfare and non-paying patients could be treated--the private hospitals refused them. Our clientele, therefore, often comprised the sickest patients. Malnutrition was common, with all its attendant health ramifications. Untreated or inadequately treated chronic disease abounded, especially among the elderly who had no other source of medical care. The working poor who came to us often had injuries or illnesses that had started out as minor, and untreated, become major. Because alcoholism ran rampant among the poor, we got more than our share of drunks with all the injuries, accidents, and illnesses to which over-indulgence makes them prone.

Not all of our patients were sick. At that time, King County Hospital also cared for obstetrical patients and their newborns, and obstetrics was a very busy department. (When the University of Washington took over the hospital's operation in the sixties, obstetrics moved to the University Medical Center.)

We employees were another part of the patient mix, receiving free care and hospitalization if necessary. The few who had insurance went elsewhere like any paying patient.

The hospital was also the trauma center for the area, so we got the nastiest accidents, and the most critically ill patients, regardless of whether they could pay. The ambulance drivers knew where to bring them—the other hospitals had emergency rooms, but were not staffed with doctors on duty 24-7 as we were.

We also received many psychiatric patients. At the time, we had the largest psychiatric unit in town. Once a week the hospital held what we loosely called the "sanity hearings." Patients were brought into the hospital a day or two beforehand or were admitted on an emergency basis specifically for the hearings that were held to determine their fate: inpatient or outpatient care, or commitment to a mental hospital. During the 1950s and 1960s, state law allowed almost anyone to swear out a warrant for someone's detention. It didn't have to be the person a patient lived with or even a relative. A judge issued the warrant if he felt the complaint was valid, and the warrant officers would bring the patient in for admission. The law also allowed emergency detention by police without going through the legal process if they found someone who appeared to be acting confused on the street or behaving "irrationally" in a way that might be a danger to himself or the public.

Unlike patients in the rest of the hospital, ability to pay was not a consideration with this group. They stayed regardless. I estimated that in the eight years I worked there, we admitted nearly 8,000 psychiatric patients. I didn't have to talk to the patients that warrant officers brought in, but for the rest, I either needed to interview them or get their information from whomever I could. Trying to interview these patients had its ups and downs. Some were relatively coherent, some not. Some gave answers that made no sense; others wouldn't even talk.

Patients with delirium tremens (DTs) went to Psychiatry. They were not as potentially dangerous as the regular psych patients could be, and were often quite docile and cooperative answering questions. However, some of their behaviors were interesting.

One evening, the nurse brought a man with DTs to my office and he sat quietly on the bench outside while I finished up with another patient. Sam, the orderly for our department, walked into my office with the man's papers. As he passed the man, he said, "Oh, oh, look out, you're sitting on a pink elephant!" The poor man jumped up and turned around, staring at the bench. He must have seen something because he wouldn't sit there again.

"That wasn't nice," I said to Sam later, although I had to control a grin.

"I know," he replied, "but I just couldn't help myself."

There were regular psychiatric patients. One was a striking woman who periodically went off the deep end and would be brought in by relatives or the police. She was tall and thin, with extraordinary black almond eyes, high cheek bones, and the streamlined body of an Olympic long distance runner.

One never knew what name she would give when she arrived. We had her cross-referenced in our files under half a dozen different first names, and even more last names. The regular nurses on all shifts knew her well, and we could always find her chart. As Bob, one of the orderlies, and I were getting off work, we saw her run out of the hospital wearing only a short hospital gown—no shoes or coat. She had somehow managed to get off the psychiatric unit with every intention to escape. We dashed to Bob's car and whipped around to follow her to try to get her back to the hospital, but she was very fleet of foot and her long legs had already carried her between buildings where the car could not go. We finally gave up, having lost her in the maze of the nearby housing development's walkways and alleys, and went about our own business. When we came back to work that night, we learned the police had found her and brought her back.

Another man came in at least once a year. Fortunately, he always gave his own name of which he was proud, being the author of some books and many articles. He taught literature at one of the local universities and every so often would become incoherent in class, sometimes throwing things at the students. During more lucid times in his life, he swore some of his best writing was done on the psychiatry unit. I've read some of his writing. Creative certainly. Articulate definitely. But lucid? (Well, I'm not the right one to judge. The interpretation of literature was one of my challenges, according to my English instructors.)

A common diagnosis for the psych patients was schizophrenia. I suspect some of them were really bipolar, but schizophrenia was the flavor of that day.

I learned quickly that the patients who had an intensity in their eyes, a boring-right-through-you quality, especially those who were diagnosed as paranoid schizophrenics, were the ones to be wary of, and at the first sign of agitation, I backed off. Of course, I learned that the hard way--with the patient who nearly escaped when I asked her religion. The eyes of those patients are burned into my memory. Over the years, I have seen a few others like that, not all of whom were headed for a psychiatric ward.

Despite the amount of attention odd behavior attracts, the psych patients were only a small part of our patient load. Many of the "ordinary" people who passed through the ER had interesting stories to tell, or were diagnostic challenges to our young interns.

THE MEDICAL STAFF

As with our clientele, I hadn't thought much about the doctors until I started working in closer association with them in the ER. Of course, there were doctors—no hospital could be without them, but didn't they just appear on their pedestals after they graduated from medical school? I hadn't wondered what life was like for the interns as just people. When I worked the night shift, there were occasions when the ER was quiet. All of us would congregate in the nurses' station and gab. It was those times I learned a lot about our new docs.

The brand-new medical school graduates burst upon the teaching hospital scene about July first of each year. Having at last earned the right to put MD after their name, they once again went from top of the medical school heap to the bottom of the resident hierarchy. In those first few days at the hospital they were bombarded with rules, procedures, schedules, and more rules--most of which they forgot until the need-to-know broke over them. An information session took up the first part of their first day in the hospital, overseen usually by the head of Medical Education and/or hospital administrator, the heads of the medical departments, and possibly various non-medical departments in some hospitals. They were given more information, and introduced to more people than they could remember, and then they were given their first assignments.

"On that first day, I was terrified," my own doctor recalled. "I kept saying over and over in my mind *I'm not ready for this!* In spite of all the clinical practice we'd had, suddenly *we* were it, and it was really frightening" When I asked him if he remembered any of his orientation meeting, he shook his head.

Dr. L.T. King wrote of his internship year in 1960-61: "King County Hospital, now Harborview, was an active and sought-after internship.... Most of us were single, and we lived at Harborview Hall, just across the street. The rooms were tiny with metal furniture, but the price was right. Uniforms, laundry, room and board were free, and the salary was $100 a month, enough for the single guys with no free time...."

Dr. King's account of his schedule was a template for the interns. "My first service was on general surgery, and I found myself and the other intern responsible for the day-to-day care of a large and busy surgical floor. Most services required every-other-night on call, and the call was usually quite busy. Our patients were quite ill and more numerous than the rooms, so many were cared for in the hall. My first chore was to write intravenous fluid orders for twenty or more patients. We also did most of the lab work ourselves and were handed the lab equipment we would need. Our experience in medical school in Iowa was quite academically oriented, and I had little practical experience. ....The learning experience was hard to beat, if strenuous."

Another doctor, whom I knew as an intern and all the way through to his becoming a board-certified specialist, said to me once, "It's a wonder we didn't kill more people. We were responsible for it all, and missed a diagnosis more often than we ever wanted to believe. There was so much we didn't know we didn't know. But I think we learned more in those days, too, because we had to rely mostly on ourselves and not on more experienced docs to bail us out like they do now. Then, too," he added, "we didn't have the lawsuit-happy patients we have today."

The end of the internship year saw the departure of some for other hospitals, and the beginning of training in specialized areas of medicine for all. There was only one physician I knew, a veteran, who decided to forego residency. "I've put my family through too much," he said. "It's time for me to earn my keep." As interns received their state license to practice at the end of that first year of residency, he opted to go into family practice in a nearby city. I often wondered how he made out without the additional two years of medical residency, or whether he went back later on.

The final paycheck for all the interns, small as it was, could be further reduced by breakage of any lab equipment issued to them at the beginning of the year, or failure to complete their medical records. Dr. King also noted, somewhat wryly, "Two weeks of vacation were promised but seldom received. For this, some additional salary was provided at the end of the year [June], and we were strongly urged to donate this largess back to the hospital."

Dr. King's comments about the environment in and around the hospital reflected how different it was then. "This was a time when illegal drugs were not much of a problem. The area at the hospital was safe and pleasant. Crime around the area where we worked and lived was minimal, and the atmosphere was rather pleasant and comforting in a way. We worked quite hard but felt together as a team with little concern for safety, malpractice claims, or danger of any sort...."

The interns and residents were a fascinating kaleidoscope of characters. In the 1950s, many were World War II veterans-- older, with far more life experience than the kids who went straight from high school through college and medical school. In terms of personality mixes, we had more difficulty with the latter than the former. But some of the veterans had more difficulty than the kids in other areas. Reactions to their new-found responsibilities (and fears) were as variable as their numbers. A few were outstanding—smart, intuitive, and with good bedside manners. Some were aggressive, while a few tried to bluff their way through. Others acknowledged their ignorance and asked for help. The good nurses, and especially the charge nurses, saved countless of these "green grassies"(*newbies*) from making critical mistakes. My friend Nancy, a surgical/critical care nurse, recalled her admonition to all the incoming interns and residents during orientation: "Listen to the nurses!"

The first week in July, therefore, was not a favorite for any of us employed in a teaching hospital. It meant new personalities, new names to learn, and a lot of patience, patience, patience. In the ER, the interns arrived, trying to show confidence instead of trepidation. It was their first time being fully responsible for cases, particularly during the night shift. To be sure, second- and third-year residents were on call if the intern got in over his head, and chief residents could be coaxed out in case they were unable to solve the problem, but I do not remember ever seeing an attending staff physician at night in King County Hospital.

Dr. King corroborated this: "Attendings were almost never present for general surgery on nights or weekends, or for that matter, any other time. Dr. Cantrell (University of Washington Medical School surgeon) arrived in the summer of 1960 and was fulltime at the hospital, made rounds with us regularly, as did Ned Brockenbrough later. If requested, they came in, but there was a tradition not to ask very often. Other 'downtown' general surgeons made rounds with us usually on Saturday mornings, but I can't recall their presence otherwise."

In the admitting office, we took bets on how long it would take the new interns to learn shorter ways of writing diagnoses on the admitting stat card. In the beginning, they spelled everything out, having been warned that abbreviations could be misinterpreted. For example, common diagnoses were myocardial infarction with congestive heart failure, or there was my favorite, full-term intrauterine pregnancy. As their first month in the ER wore on, we would begin to see MI/CHF, and FTIUP. And as the diagnoses got more abbreviated, the handwriting deteriorated. One intern tried to do us a favor by printing because his handwriting was so bad; however, his printing was often illegible, too. Sometimes even the intern who'd written it couldn't read it after a day or two. Gradually, we all became quite expert at deciphering.

With all the new experiences, brutal schedules, and nerve-wracking responsibilities, the new—mostly male—interns were also subject to the scrutiny of the young, single nurses, some of whom were new graduates themselves. Who was married and who was single was another game played during those first months with the new interns. During my first years there, many were WWII veterans and already married, which reduced the game-playing and distractions--at least for them.

In addition to all the other things these new kids on the block had to contend with, there were occasional bits of mischief dreamed up by the evening and night shift employees, sometimes including other interns or residents. They were harmless, but designed to take the wind out of sails too puffed up, or sometimes simply offered a little break in the routine when things were slow.

Andy was one of our regular orderlies who worked evenings on the psychiatric unit. He had rather peculiar physiology, with an unusually low blood pressure of about 60/40. The textbook-normal blood pressure is significantly higher, 120/80, so at first glance Andy's blood pressure looked like that of a patient in shock. His natural skin color was almost blue-white, in sharp contrast to his black hair, all of which aided in the deception of innocent interns.

Andy's modus operandi was simple. When he judged that one of the new interns was ripe for victimization, he would put his head in his hands, and say very softly, "I don't feel so good."

When his intended victim looked up or asked him what was wrong, Andy would stand up, stagger a few steps, and then fall to his knees or collapse back into a chair, looking terribly weak and faint. It was usually then the intern noticed for the first time how pale he was. Andy would be put quickly into a wheelchair and whisked off to the ER sometimes with the intern in tow.

Depending upon patient load and who the charge nurse was that night, the deception might end there, with a sharp "Andy, get up and go back to work." But if the Emergency intern was also the target and the nurses were in on it, they would let it continue. His low blood pressure would get the intern all excited, especially when Andy was lying down. (Lying or supine blood pressure is usually "normal," whereas when changing position from supine to sitting or standing, blood pressures can go down significantly in a number of conditions.) Although the interns were aware of normal variations in blood pressure, they were often taken aback by Andy's readings. Of course, this only worked a couple of times with the new crop, after which the word got around and Andy's fun was over.

Sometimes we didn't have to do anything to initiate a new intern: we had a regular among the patients who often provided the new interns in the ER an introduction to street behavior. This was Lenny, our chronic epileptic. He was about 40, rather emaciated, with thinning dishwater-blond hair. We would see him periodically when he drank too much, a no-no for an epileptic, predictably at the beginning of the cold season when sleeping on the street was no longer comfortable. He usually arrived by police car, sometimes by ambulance, having managed to convince someone on the street that he was having a seizure. When he came in by car, he would sit in a waiting room chair and shake so that he appeared to be having a seizure. He was such a regular customer that he only had to walk through the door and I could go right to his chart in our files.

When Lenny came in on foot and started his act in a chair, the new intern would see Lenny start to shake, and say something like, "Get him into a room now."

This was usually a job for Sam, our regular orderly. Being well-versed in Lenny's routine, he would whisper to the intern, "Watch this." Then he would go over to the patient and say, "Hey, Lenny, want a drink of water?" and Lenny would stop his shaking, sit up and say, "Sure." (I must confess, we all felt he had to be several slices short of a full loaf to fall for that every time.)

At this point, the intern understood, and would turn away, sometimes irritated, to go about his business, and Sam and the nurses (and the rest of us) would chuckle. And Lenny would have to take his turn with the rest of the patients.

The young doctors sometimes added to the mischief—usually on the night shift. One surgical intern, Frank, a tall, skinny, slightly hyperactive man, had a difficult time when things were slow. He would pace for a while, and then, usually in collusion with an orderly, concoct some plot. On one night that sticks in my mind Frank plopped himself onto an empty stretcher. The orderly strapped him down and Frank, kicking and shouting, pretended to be one of our "certifiable" patients. The orderly whisked him up the elevator to the psychiatric unit, Frank struggling to "escape" and carrying on, until they woke up any staff who was misguided enough to think about sleeping just because the patients were. After raising an adequately satisfying ruckus, the pair returned, chortling and energized, ready to take on any new arrivals in the Emergency Room.

To the best of my knowledge, such high jinks went unreported to supervisors or the staff physicians who oversaw the education of house staff—although I suspect most of them would have simply smiled.

HOWARD

The difference between the interns who had seen more of life before going to medical school, and the younger ones who went straight from high school through college and medical school was sometimes stark. The older ones were more goal-directed, exhibited more maturity in dealing with a diverse population, and complained less. The younger ones often griped about the long hours and were less adept in dealing with our low-income group, especially those patients for whom English was a second language. Nor did the patients react as well to the young ones. One patient, encountering an intern of the latter group who looked like he was about sixteen, refused to be examined by him, saying, "I want to see a real doctor."

Howard, however, was about thirty-three years old and a WWII veteran like many of the residents those days. He'd gone through medical school on the GI Bill. Mature and dedicated to his profession, he had a deep interest in his patients. Of medium height, well-muscled and fit, Howard responded to the punishing hours meted out to first year interns without complaint. Because he had taken to heart the admonition "listen to the nurses," he came through his first couple of weeks in the ER that December without any major *faux pas*.

Christmas Eve of 1953 was unnaturally quiet in the ER. In all the years I worked there, I don't recall another night when we had **no** patients between midnight and 6 AM in the morning. When 1:00

46

AM had come and gone without so much as a nearby siren, Howard yawned, stretched sleepily, and went to lie down on one of the beds in the Recovery Room next to my office.

Overlooking the small ambulance court, the Recovery Room--a total misnomer--had four squeaky, iron-framed cots, separated by white curtains between the beds for a modicum of privacy. If a vehicle came in, Howard was confident he would wake up quickly, and so he pulled the curtain and dozed off.

Within the next hour, without even a phone call, I poured myself into the next bed over, followed shortly by the orderly in the third bed. Hazel, the elderly night charge nurse, catnapped quietly in a chair at the nurses' station. Night shifters never get enough sleep.

About 6 AM in the morning, our first patient of the day arrived. The orderly and I had by that time arisen, I to catch up on the morning book work, and he to straighten up the offices and examining rooms. Howard, however, slept soundly until the clatter of activity awakened him. He rolled off the bed, fully alert and ready for action in one seamless move, finger-combing his dark-brown hair to restore a more ordered appearance.

The next night, Christmas, when I came back on duty, Howard pulled me aside and with a big grin said, "I told my wife I slept with the admitting clerk last night."

I laughed. "Rat! I suppose she wouldn't think of kicking you out on Christmas. Or did she just kick you?" He waggled his eyebrows and went off to see a patient.

But it was this same mischievous Howard who nearly quit medicine completely a few days later. A patient arrived one afternoon in great pain and very short of breath. He was having so much difficulty breathing that he could hardly say a word unless he was sitting straight up. He was also having severe chest pain and his eyes were wide and frightened. After Howard had examined him and ordered an EKG, he diagnosed a myocardial infarction (heart attack) and admitted him stat. The orderly got the patient onto a stretcher, strapped down so he wouldn't fall off, and then Howard went out to write orders on the patient's chart. The nurse brought me the chart, and I called the floor to let them know the patient was on his way. Howard went on to another patient.

A minute or two went by and I heard some muttering by one of the nurses and a call for Howard to come look at the cardiac patient. I saw the stretcher with the patient stop briefly just outside my office, and the nurse, obviously trying to control her irritation, told Howard, "You have to stay with a patient in this condition until he is taken care of, doctor." With this, she grabbed a wooden chair and telling Howard to pull the patient up to a sitting position, propped the chair behind the stretcher pad. "Patients with MI's often have pulmonary edema, and they'll drown in their own fluid if you leave them lying flat." Together they raced the patient to the floor, and fortunately, due to the nurse's quick action, he made it there alive. Howard finished out his shift quite subdued.

I got the rest of the story the next night. After he got off shift, Howard had gone to the administrator's office and told him he was quitting medicine. He wasn't smart enough to be a doctor and couldn't handle endangering patients with the kind of error he had made last night. He saw a dismal future--his education was all for naught and he wondered what he could do now. The scuttlebutt was it took the administrator quite some time to convince Howard that one mistake was not the end of his career as a physician, and indeed, he was going to be a much better one for having so much concern for his patients. What else he said only they knew, but Howard did not leave the profession.

Although I never got to know the interns and residents nearly as well as did the nurses who worked directly with them, Howard remained one of the special ones. He talked to everyone, and remembered their names regardless of position. The patients warmed to him readily, as he did to them. We all missed him when he rotated out of the ER. I don't know where he finally went to practice after his residency was completed, but his patients were lucky to have him.

A NECESSARY ANNOYANCE

In those days of paper records, the Medical Records Department (MRD) was considered necessary but bothersome: necessary because that was where the patient records were maintained, and a bother because the doctors had to go there to complete their charts.

What constituted completion[2] by physicians was determined by medical staff committees, and administered by the MRD. Dereliction of duty had consequences, though not severe for the house staff at King County Hospital. In private hospitals, consistent failure to complete records meant the attending physician could be temporarily removed from staff and unable to admit patients--a potential monetary handicap, especially for surgeons. Their business was operating, which could only be done in a hospital, and so there went the yacht! Of course, all they had to do was repent (i.e., complete their charts) and all was forgiven—until the next time they sinned.[3]

At King County Hospital, however, such disciplinary measures were impractical and therefore not done, though the interns and residents could be in hot water with their attending faculty physicians for not completing charts. As noted before, such failure could have a monetary impact on the resident's last paycheck of the academic year.

For the doctors, missing signatures were picky details that didn't affect the care they had given. Coming down to the Medical Records

Department was an annoyance, particularly if it was only for such things.

We all became inured to the irritated mutterings of the occasional doctor, or the chastisement if the right chart couldn't be found. One MRD evening supervisor, however, became incensed at a resident who, working on a large pile of charts, threw each one on the floor when he was finished with it.

"Young man," she said sternly, "that is NOT how you treat medical records! They are not to be thrown around."

This blackguard, however, merely looked at her and instead of throwing the next one down, slowly and delicately placed it on the floor on top of those already strewn about. My memory says she reported him, but I doubt anything happened as a result.

Everyone working swing and night shifts was accustomed to being hailed by a doctor working on his charts, complaining about something. "This isn't my patient." "I didn't write that order." "Dr. X discharged this patient." The complaint was duly noted and referred back to the clerk in charge of the incomplete files.

Certainly, mistakes were sometimes made in assigning the charts to the right doctor, made more complicated by their rotation off-service before their patient was discharged. At the end of the year, if an intern or resident left the hospital without completing his charts, the chief resident or (gasp!) the attending faculty physician was responsible for signing off. One does not need much imagination to know how that was received. One resident, who was leaving the state, was rumored to have taken all his incomplete charts out of the hospital and thrown them away. To the best of my knowledge that batch was never found.

All doctors want the best, most accurate, relevant information on the patients they see—if only they didn't have to spend so much time providing it themselves.

One function of the Medical Records Department met with far less frustration, however: research. Because of the detailed coding and indexing of diseases and operations maintained by the department, a physician could request charts to be pulled for nearly anything. Although rarely did an intern have any time for research, as one got higher up in the pecking order, such things became possible. Faculty physicians also made requests. There were almost always several piles of charts, each with a sign on top, saying, for example, "Dr. Jones – Gallbladder Study." Requests could come from other sources such as nursing or administration, but these were far less frequent.

Just before the new wing opened in 1955, a microfilm program was initiated, and all death charts and records of patients who had not been seen in a long time were filmed on 35 mm reels. Research involving any of those records required notifying the department ahead of time so that the appropriate reel(s) could be retrieved and set up for the requestor. The readers were cumbersome and, uniformly, the doctors hated anything to do with microfilm. In later years, when I was put in charge of a microfilm program in another hospital, the head of the Department of Medicine, whom I had known as a resident at King County Hospital, fought it fist and claw, until I promised there would be no reels. Fortunately the technology had advanced sufficiently by then so that no one was using them.

For doctors who chose to give their hands a rest, reports such as histories and physicals, consultations and discharge summaries could be dictated, and it was required for operative reports. Compared to the digital equipment we have now, the dictation machines were primitive, with a hand-held microphone attached. The dictation equipment used small discs the size of the old forty-five records. Several were available in the department, and others were scattered on the different inpatient floors. At the end of each day, completed discs were brought to the transcriptionists in the department. Voice fidelity was not the shining characteristic of the machines of that era, and my hat is off to the women who were able to decipher the mutterings of tired doctors dictated into persnickety machines onto scratchy records. A couple of medical secretaries who took shorthand were assigned to the physician in charge of obstetrics/gynecology and to surgery, but the high cost of skilled labor limited such positions.

In all the books I have read written by doctors, only one or two made any mention of even being aware of the Medical Records Department. Whether they loved it, hated it, or merely put up with it, the department was—and is—an integral part of medical staff existence.

NANCY

"Mind if I join you?" I was in the small night coffee shop, which was crowded at the 2 a.m. hour. Jim, an orderly I knew, sat with Megan, an OB nurse, and another nurse I didn't know.

"Please do," Megan replied, and as I sat down, she said, "Do you know Nancy? She was my roommate at Seattle U. She just started working up on 9-Center."

That was my first encounter with the woman who became one of my best friends. After that night we met often in the coffee shop and quickly got well acquainted.

When she first started work, she was assigned as a float, but was now settled on the postoperative ward, working with the surgeons. Even as a 22-year-old new graduate, Nancy was a commanding figure. At five feet, ten inches, she was taller than most of the nurses and some of the physicians. With black hair and a big-boned, heavy-busted frame, she exuded an aura of authority long before she was promoted into a position where she was allowed to use it. But her brown eyes twinkled often and her laughter was hearty and spontaneous. Her full lips and straight white teeth made her smile a dentist's dream, and lit up many a patient's room. Her long legs carried her with purposeful stride down the ward's long hallway whenever a patient needed her during the night. Nancy was a welcome sight to sick and hurting people.

One night in the coffee shop, we were both a bit tired and ran out of work gossip. After a short silence, I asked what made her decide on nursing. She laughed. "I made that decision when I was six. Never changed. Remember those doctor kits, the ones with a little stethoscope and sugar pills? We used to play doctor in grade school."

"But how did you ever get from Montana to Seattle U? Didn't they have any nursing schools there?"

"The summer before my senior year in high school, I came to visit my dad in Seattle, and got a job in the kitchen at Providence. The director asked me if I was interested in nursing because Seattle U was trying to recruit blacks for their program. I was offered a scholarship at a small college in Montana, but I didn't want to face the isolation and the horrible cold winters anymore, so I registered for SU when I got back to Helena."

Nancy's mother died when she was only eighteen months old and because her father was an orchard worker in Eastern Washington, she was raised by his mother in Helena, Montana. Her grandmother's influence was reflected in her good manners, her love of good food, and her strong moral sense.

The patients were always the focus of her attention and concern. "I've always been an advocate for the patient," she told me. If she barked at staff, it was because the patients needed their attention and weren't getting it. If she ordered a patient around, it was because he was doing something not in his own best interests. Certain staff members were chronically irritated with Nancy, but the nurses who shared her dedication worked well with her.

She commented to me one day at coffee, "When you're black, you have to be twice as good as white people at what you do." With Nancy, skin color wasn't something anyone paid attention to, because she *was* twice as good as any other nurse I knew.

Nancy

TRAGEDIES AND NEAR MISSES

By the beginning of 1954, I was in ER admitting four out of five days a week, relieving the day and evening shift clerks, and once in awhile, the night shift clerk. Work was never dull.

One morning, I came on duty to find everyone buzzing about the night's events. The night admitting clerk, Ellen, didn't even bother to say hello. Her first words to me were, "Did you hear? A patient jumped out of an upper story window and landed on the fence."

"Oh, my God, did he survive?" The vision I had immediately was grim. It was a spiked fence, okay from an architectural standpoint, but not friendly to a falling body.

"Not hardly! It was awful. Nobody knows why he jumped."

Fortunately, maintenance had already cleaned up the area and the rest of the day was blessedly normal.

Another morning the ambulance drivers came roaring in from a bad car accident. An elderly woman had been injured. They brought her in and transferred her to the ER gurney, rolling her over when they did so. She cried out in pain.

"You know you're not supposed to roll patients over who've been in accidents!" The nurse glared at them as she brought the patient into the first examining room. "She could have broken ribs, for heaven's sake."

57

The ambulance attendants had the good grace to look sheepish. As soon as possible, they called me in to get her registered. Not long afterward, the chief surgical resident came down to see her and we discovered she was his mother-in-law. He was calm and as gentle as possible in his examination, reassuring her everything would be done to ease her pain and help her through this. He had the reputation of suturing wounds with the skill of a sewing machine: even, close, and delicate. He stayed with her and escorted her directly to the operating room. The diagnosis he wrote on her stat card was "Flail chest, punctured right lung." Unfortunately, she died several days later of complications. Was it the ambulance crew's fault? Maybe not, but the punctured lung from the broken ribs certainly didn't help.

Near misses happened, too. Late one afternoon during the winter, one of the maintenance men walked through the ER carrying a hose that was all wrapped up. No one noticed him at the time. Maintenance and engineering staff frequently wandered through with tools and other equipment. It was a busy night without much time to pay attention to anything but our own jobs. Midway through the evening, after delivering a patient, an ambulance driver came back in and asked the charge nurse, "Anybody know how long that car's been running out here?"

The nurse went to the driver's side door, took one look, and ran back in.

"Sam, bring a gurney, quick." The orderly grabbed the one near the door, while the nurse ran to the car and yanked off a hose running from the exhaust pipe into the window. Between the three of them, they got the driver's door open, pulled the unconscious man onto the cart, and pushed it into the ER. One of them turned off the car's engine.

We all knew he worked in maintenance, but no one knew his name. The nurse called the Maintenance Department's evening supervisor, who came immediately. Once identified, he brought the man's personnel file and I was able to get the basic information we needed to determine he already had a chart and to notify the relative he had listed. While his first blood work was obtained, they administered oxygen, and then he was admitted stat.

This patient survived and was sent to psychiatry after he recovered. Fortunately he had no significant impairment from his carbon monoxide poisoning, but it was quite a long time before he returned to work.

In the 1950s, Boeing Aircraft Company was converting from war-time plane manufacturing to relative peace-time, although the Cold War was in its early stages. The Defense Department orders for planes slowed and Boeing had massive lay-offs. Locally, it was disastrous because Boeing was the largest employer in the area at the time. The spill-over to lay-offs by local suppliers and workers made the impact huge. One evening between Thanksgiving and Christmas, we were witnesses to the result of one laid-off worker's despair.

Ambulances brought in a father and son. The man had been laid off for some time and had been unable to find work. He had killed his wife and one of his children. He had beaten another son to unconsciousness with a baseball bat, fracturing his skull. Then he had filled a tub with warm water, slashed his arms and wrists in a pattern that produced rectangular flaps of skin, and climbed into the tub to bleed to death. Neighbors had heard the screams and called for help.

While the doctor was suturing his extensive wounds, I was able to get what little information I could from this desperately depressed man. The boy was admitted to the operating room stat. I have never seen a skull which looked like that: it appeared dented. One could actually see the outline of the bat. The boy was fortunately not conscious, and I don't know whether he survived. His father did. Not surprisingly, during that Boeing downturn such incidents increased--although none quite like this one.

Another evening, an ambulance arrived with a warrant officer whom we knew well, Peter. The attendant told us Peter had been sent to pick up a patient due for evaluation at the weekly psychiatric hearings. The patient was known to be violent, so Peter had talked to the father, who assured him his son (the patient) was unarmed. The son lived in a separate house on the father's property out in the county. When Peter and another officer had gone there, the son had opened fire on them, killing the other man and wounding Peter.

Unfortunately, one of the ER nurses, Miriam, had been dating Peter and she was on duty when they brought him in. A quick evaluation by the doctor revealed that he had died, probably en route to the hospital. Miriam maintained her composure throughout the long evening, but fled immediately after her shift.

The perpetrator of this tragedy was brought in later, in handcuffs. Perhaps not fairly, most of us felt anger toward the father and the patient, but we could not allow ourselves the luxury of showing it. Keeping a lid on emotions, especially negative ones, was a lesson I learned well in the ER.

Although the police were frequent visitors to ER, because they had insurance coverage they were seldom patients. However, one who had been involved in a shooting downtown was brought in badly wounded. The officer was in surgery for several hours. The police chief was so concerned he kept calling to find out the man's condition, and insisted on speaking only to the surgeon. This meant Dr. J. had to come out of surgery and then scrub up again each time. When he finally finished the surgery, it was after three in the morning. He came down to the little coffee room that opened after the night café closed, plopped down in a chair with a cup of coffee, and told those of us present about "all the nonsense."

"I finally told the chief that if he didn't stop calling me out of surgery, the man probably *would* die." He rolled his eyes and shook his head. "I don't know what it takes to make these guys understand it's not like interrupting someone having a beer. He wouldn't have died, but I had to get the guy off my back. It took a lot of time to get the bullets out and get him sewed back together. Cops!"

DIGGER

Digger was a hospital orderly. We called him that after Digger Odell, the funeral director of an old radio show. He earned his name due, in equal parts, to his build, a somewhat distorted sense of humor, and some unfortunate timing. I don't think anyone even remembered his real name.

He usually worked on one of the medical floors, but when our regular orderly was absent, Digger was occasionally assigned to Emergency. He stood six feet five inches, thin to the point of barely casting a shadow in bright light, and had a nose that some generously called "aquiline"—a term that did not adequately describe its heroic proportions. He had thick, straight black hair and skin that was almost blue-white. With an appearance of one who never saw the sun, it seemed appropriate that he worked the night shift.

The first time I encountered Digger was a hot, midsummer night. The small ER waiting room was full of angry, frustrated people. Some were patients, some were relatives of patients. As Digger came on shift at 11 PM, he just had time to take report from the orderly going off duty before the entry doors burst open and ambulance attendants rushed in with a man on a stretcher, covered with blood. Digger was right there to help the ambulance attendant and a nurse move the man onto the ER stretcher. As he did so, a clot-like substance that seemed the size of a liver fell onto the floor. The nurse shouted for one of the doctors as she and Digger pushed the patient into the treatment room. The man had been stabbed in the abdomen; the wound so big it looked like it had been made with a butcher knife. I grabbed my clipboard and a registration card and followed them into the room, dodging the "clot" on the floor, to try to get identifying information, although it was clear that would have to wait. A flurry of activity preceded the man's admission directly to the operating room, and finally Digger was able to take care of the blood or whatever it was on the floor.

That event set the pace for the night. It was one bloody mess after another, whether from car accidents, knife fights, or shootings. Digger was right in the middle of the on-going mayhem, racing patients to X-Ray, the operating room, or to other floors, cleaning up blood from anywhere and everywhere, as well as other, even less savory messes. (The night "environmental sanitation" staff were seldom anywhere to be found when you needed them.)

Digger was good in a crunch. He knew what was needed and did it, often anticipating the nurse's or doctor's orders. He would have made a good Medic had that program been available then. A number of patients actually owed their lives to his quick thinking or the speed he could generate with those long legs. Once he even delivered a baby—the mother's fifth--in the elevator, which was far too slow for the boy, who was in a hurry.

Still, why was it that the worst, messiest cases always came in when he was on duty in ER? Perhaps it was simply coincidence or perhaps the night supervisor had some prescience about the nights she assigned him to the Emergency Department. Either way, it became such a pattern that whenever he appeared for work, we all groaned. Sure enough, it would be a grim night.

In addition to that, his sense of humor was almost Dickensian. The dark hallways of the hospital at night provided him with the grist for his practical jokes. He had a penchant for appearing suddenly out of the shadows, long arms raised over his head, a true Elizabethan apparition, hugely enjoying the moment of terror engendered in his unsuspecting victim. Women were his most frequent targets, and we lowly clerical types were especially delectable game; we shrieked much more satisfyingly than the more sanguine nurses, although on occasion he even achieved a sudden indrawn breath from one of them.

He pulled his phantom act on me one morning about 2:30 AM as I went through a doorway into the darkened main corridor on my way to the coffee shop. I let out a terrified squeak.

"Gotcha!" he grinned.

Of course, this was not an every night event or it would have lost its punch. But of the three shifts, nights had the most variability in work load, so occasional mischief was possible. Digger made the most of it.

Apart from his odd sense of humor and his obvious skills, we knew very little about Digger. He was uncomfortable talking to people, especially women. His practical jokes seemed a way of interacting sociably without giving away much of the inner man. He kept to himself when he wasn't busy, and didn't seem to have any close friends, even among the other men.

Eventually I realized I hadn't seen Digger for a while, and I asked our regular orderly where he was.

"Oh, he quit. Went to San Francisco," came the reply.

Did he go into another line of work? If he stayed with hospitals, did the circumstances repeat themselves there? Did he perhaps use his experience to further his education and increase his skills? I quietly hoped things went well for him. Beneath his rather unusual appearance and his practical jokes, I suspect there existed a shy man who wanted a normal life. I hope he found it.

THE OLD SPICE BOTTLE

We all make mistakes. Some are critical, some embarrassing, some barely noteworthy. They happen as often in hospitals as anywhere else.

Late one night, a middle-aged and rather corpulent gentleman waddled in, complaining of pain in his low back. After obtaining his basic information, the nurse took him into an examining room and told him to have a seat. He politely declined and continued to stand. When the doctor came it, the patient asked the nurse to leave so he could talk to the doctor alone. Later, after the patient had left, and there was a momentary lull in business, I heard a great deal of chuckling and came out to find out what was amusing everyone.

After the nurse left the room, the patient with the "lower back pain" had confessed that it was really rectal pain. He told the intern that he had come out of the shower and had lathered up to shave. His bathroom, he explained, was very small and had no counter, so he had put the shaving cream bottle on the toilet seat.

"Then I slipped, and fell backwards onto the shaving cream bottle, and it got shoved up…there." He gestured to his rear. "I couldn't get it out."

Somehow, the intern maintained his composure, and as gently as he could, removed the offending bottle of shaving cream.

"Must have been a *really* small bathroom," I commented.

"Oh, come on," the intern said, "You don't actually think I bought *that*, do you?"

And we all burst out laughing about the Old Spice bottle.

WHEN IN NEED, A FRIEND IN DEED

Dick was one of the orderlies with whom we ER staff especially liked to work. He knew the routines in emergency, as well as those on all the patient floors. The nursing supervisors, who scheduled the orderlies, could place him anywhere with confidence. He floated between evening and night shifts, as did I, so we often found ourselves working together. His wife was a nurse who worked days at another hospital. I wondered why he chose to work a different shift, but it was none of my business.

Dick was a small man, no taller than five-feet-six or -seven inches. Because he was thin as a toothpick and weighed a little over 120 pounds, he seemed even shorter. He was quiet though not really shy; he chose when he wanted to say something, and didn't make small talk. Nevertheless, his changing facial expressions showed he was obviously engaged in conversations flowing around him. On occasion, his blue eyes twinkled as though at a secret joke, or contemplating some mischief. Not a demonstrative person, he had his own unique ways of showing concern for people.

Dick was on duty September 1, 1954, the day Nazir and our daughter, Nish, just eighteen months old, left Seattle with one-way tickets to England. When I came to work that afternoon, he made no comment about my swollen red eyes and asked no questions. As business slacked off around ten o'clock, he came into my office and sat down.

"Talk to me," he said.

It was so unexpected, and I was so raw and in need of a friend, that, drippy-eyed, I told him more than he probably wanted to know.

By August, the final nails in the coffin of my marriage had been hammered home. Nazir was awarded custody of our daughter, Nish, although I had unlimited privileges. I knew he could provide for her much better than I could, as I could barely pay for child care on my meager salary. I had not expected him to leave Seattle, but did not know how I could stop him. From that day, my beautiful black-haired, brown-eyed daughter was gone from my life.

Dick listened without comment as I wound to a stop.

"Better?"

"Better," I acknowledged, finding to my surprise that I really was.

A few days later, Dick and I worked a Friday night shift together. About six-thirty Saturday morning, he leaned against the office door, as I finished typing the night reports.

"How would you like to go to the Puyallup fair today?"

"Right after work?" I had to think about that for a moment. "Does your wife want to go?"

"No, she has to work today."

"Won't she mind?"

"No, she doesn't like fairs anyway—too crowded and too much walking."

After breakfast at the hospital and a quick trip to our respective homes to change clothes, we went to the fair and I forgot about my daughter for a while. We had a good time, and Dick found a creative jeweler's display, which made it all worthwhile for him. His hobby was working with gold and silver to make rings, pins, and other jewelry. When I finally got home and poured myself into bed, I wondered if that day had been his version of therapy, or if I was interpreting it way beyond reality. I chose to take it as the former.

Then, late one afternoon in October, a tiny girl with black wavy hair, dark eyes, and a big smile, walked into the office hand-in-hand with an older woman, identified as a guardian ad litem. Her chart said she was four years old, though she was not much bigger than my daughter who had left a month before. The resemblance to Nish caught me by surprise, and for a minute or two, I could only stare, mouth open, not even breathing. Dick, on duty that afternoon, waved his hand in front of my face.

"Hey, are you in there? She's going to peds."

The dysfunction passed, and I returned to the job at hand. As I typed, the little girl slid off the woman's lap and came behind the desk to watch.

"What are you doing?" she asked, pointing to the typewriter.

"I'm typing up your information, Miss Emily," I replied, smiling down at this bubbly child.

"My name's Emmy," she corrected, pertly. Then she turned to the steel cupboard against the wall. "What's in there?"

"Lots of paper and stuff for the office."

"Can I see?" She looked at me over her shoulder with those big brown, long-lashed eyes that would reduce even a Minotaur to jelly.

"Now, Emmy," her companion said, "Don't ask so many questions." The woman smiled apologetically at me. "She's such an inquisitive child."

"No problem," I replied, as I pulled the completed stat card out of the typewriter.

Reaching over to the cupboard, I opened it and retrieved a blank sheet of paper. "How would you like to type something?"

70

Emmy excitedly tugged at my skirt, and I plopped her onto my lap so she could reach the keys. Like any child, she pushed hard on the keyboard, one finger at a time, then with her whole palm, and, of course, the keys stuck together, the jam increasing as she pressed more letters. She stopped and looked up at me, anxiously.

"Did I break it?"

"No. It just has to be untangled. Here," I said, extracting the paper, and producing a pencil from the desk drawer, "why don't you draw me a picture?"

While she busied herself with her new task, I called pediatrics, to let them know their planned admission from Yakima was here. She was being admitted for heart surgery, though I don't recall the exact diagnosis. She did not appear ill, but I noticed the extreme paleness of her fingers and nail beds, almost cyanotic (blue), and she seemed short of breath just walking around the room.

"Come on, young lady, let's go for a ride." Dick reappeared at the door, this time with a wheelchair. She dropped the pencil and jumped to the floor, eager for this new experience. She looked even smaller in the big wooden contraption.

As they left, I wondered what my daughter would be like at Emmy's age. Would life with her father allow for such spontaneous curiosity? Would I ever have the chance to see her again and find out? That thought made me turn away when Dick came back to the office. Grabbing a tissue, I blotted my eyes to stave off the impending flood. Dick sat quietly. I cleared my throat and turned around.

"That was a little too close for comfort," I said.

Dick looked at me closely, and then simply nodded. He had been so supportive through that difficult shift a month ago, I knew he understood.

Our friendship blossomed, but remained within the confines of work. Two years later, when I married again, Dick made our wedding rings, a simple elegant design in silver, with a matching pair of earrings for me. Although he rarely attended the outside activities of our group, he remained a special part of my "work family."

LIFE GOES ON

When I first separated from Nazir, I moved into a one-room apartment with a hot plate; the refrigerator and bath down the hall was shared with other roomers. By the next month, I found a one-room apartment, with Murphy bed and a complete, if tacked on, kitchen and bath.

Away from work, I was a bit lonely and started frequenting the People's Center, a non-denominational church with rooms on its street level that were rented out to university students. Just two blocks from our old apartment, it was run by the church's minister, father of my close friend, Ruth. The Center hosted dances, and other social events, which Nazir and I had attended often, so I knew most of its residents.

I had met B. Robert, an anthropology student who lived at the Center, while Nazir and I were still married. Now Bob and I had the chance to get better acquainted, and I met him often for coffee and conversation. Once headed for pre-med, a field trip had turned his interest to archeology and he'd never looked back. Although he was a Navy veteran, his GI Bill funds were proving inadequate and he needed a job.

"Why don't you apply at the hospital?" I suggested to him.

He took me up on it and was hired as an orderly. On the days we worked the same shift, we went to work together, and it wasn't too long before we decided it would be cheaper if we found our own place and split the rent. In April of 1954, we moved into an apartment two blocks from campus. The move was primarily economic, although I was happy to have a man in my life again. Having just left a contentious relationship, I was leery about entanglements and Bob was happy to be rid of the two roommates with whom he had little in common. (Nazir had moved in with a young mother, also in the process of getting a divorce.)

B. Robert was sandy-haired and blue-eyed, and as brilliant a man as I had ever met. His I.Q, he told me, quite modestly, was 154. Intellectual brilliance, however, does not always extend to social acumen, and Bob was not an exception. He delighted in being the contrarian in discussions, and although he always made his comments with a smile and a laugh, he managed to irritate other participants-- especially those in his chosen field.

Working and living together was sometimes a trial—too much togetherness. He complained about my cooking, my tendency toward procrastination, and what he perceived as my negative attitude: I complained about his complaining. On one occasion, when I expressed my guilt over leaving Nish, he said, "You made the decision. Get over it." After that I kept such things to myself. He could be a prickly roommate but our arguments at home did not carry over to work, and we had enough good times to balance out the differences.

With my divorce final and B. Robert's urging me "not to procrastinate any more," I registered for classes at the university, determined to finish my degree. We settled into routines: nights at work, days in classes, and a few hours of sleep.

Over coffee one morning, B. Robert leaned back in his chair, hands laced behind his head, and said with a grin, "Why don't we get married and you can support me through grad school?"

Remembering all the financial arguments that arose with Nazir, it took me all of a minute to say, "Thanks, but I don't think so."

In March of 1955, I moved out and back into my father's home. Big changes were happening at work, too. That same month, the new wing of the hospital was opened.

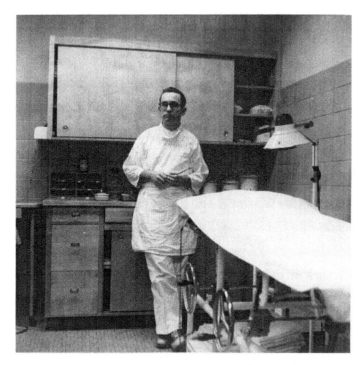

B. Robert in examining room of new wing.

CULTURE CHANGE

The original Medical Records Department was crowded, lined with file cabinets and desks and tables overflowing with charts and papers. There was barely enough room to navigate around the people sitting at desks. Small, below-sidewalk windows were best forgotten—light barely filtered through the years of accumulated dirt and added construction dust. When the file drawers were open, the aisles were impassable. The Emergency Room was also small, given the volume of patients. Everything was close together with inadequate space.

Nevertheless, in both departments there was a feeling that we were all in it together, which promoted the camaraderie Dr. King noted. In the ER, we were in each other's pockets most of the time, and in quiet moments, we hung out together: doctors, nurses, admitting clerk, orderly—the whole "family." Granted, with all of us in the nursing station, we had to be careful not to stand on each other's toes. Still, the cozy informality provided the opportunity for us non-medical types to learn a lot about medicine and its practice in a way far better than in the classroom. The atmosphere was comfortable and friendly, with rare exceptions. When a patient arrived, we knew at once, and scampered back to our respective "homes."

Then progress overtook us. When the new wing opened in March, 1955, we were all in heaven: an expansive ground floor with a Screening Clinic for new patients; the Medical Records Department was huge (by comparison), with a large wall of *clean* windows above-ground, and a lower level file room big enough to hold all the patient records instead of just six months' worth. A pneumatic tube system meant much more efficient transport of charts to the new clinics and to the ER.

Best of all, from the standpoint of the staff, the ER was greatly expanded with one real critical care room, seven regular examining rooms, a nurses station big enough for six or seven people to mill about, rather than being overcrowded with four, and an eight-bed observation ward.

Instead of one recycled wooden desk, two chairs, and a steel cupboard, the new admitting office sported two brand-new metal desks, four chairs, a built-in cupboard, coat rack, and a separate, glassed-in, soundproofed room for a ditto machine (hurray—fewer carbons!). The office was all windows, and overlooked the new parking lot. It felt like the size of a football field in comparison to the old cramped space. We now had an intercom, which connected us to the ER nursing station and Medical Records, and other departments. A large waiting room just outside the office boasted a long wooden bench and for some reason, a wash basin reappeared adjacent to the outside wall.

Moreover, with the move into the new building, X-Ray had been relocated to the same floor as the Emergency Department, much closer than the previous second floor location, which had made urgent x-rays dependent on the availability and speed of an ancient elevator. We hardly knew what to do with ourselves in all that space.

But almost immediately I did miss one thing: the intimate closeness of the old ER. Now the admitting office was down the hall about fifty feet from the nurses station, which seemed like a hundred, and we felt much more isolated. Unlike the old arrangement, the orderly and I often did not know what was happening in the main part of the ER unless we went down there to see. Communication was mostly by intercom from the nurses to us, rather than a call around the corner. We all had to make changes for "progress," we were told, and this really was much more efficient for patient care. But something ephemeral and special was lost in translation.

The orderlies, however, really loved their own office next to admitting, which boasted a real desk instead of the small, old left-over table. Two curtained-off bathtubs with showers and a changing room for the patients added luxury--although it was unclear just when or under what circumstances these would be used.

It was on one of those early nights in our wonderful new wing when I got a call over the intercom to register a new patient in room three. Even before I got there, I could smell him. Working in the ER, one gets used to all kinds of odors, so, clipboard in hand, I mentally held my nose and went in. When I got to "occupation" on the stat card, it did not surprise me when the patient replied "fisherman." For reasons known only to them, it was our experience that the men in this line of work year-round seemed to regard water as something for fish to swim in, but not to wash in. Of course, this was not all fishermen, but we got an inordinate number from this group who seemed to regard bathing as a once-a-year event. This man, by whiff, fit that category.

As I came out, Dr. Madison, the ER intern on duty, was on her way to the treatment room. This was her first week in Emergency and she was not yet used to the routines of the department or comfortable dealing with the patients who made up the bulk of our clientele. She wrinkled her nose. "What is that god-awful smell?"

"He's a fisherman." I showed her the name on the stat card I had just completed.

She opened the door and waved a hand in front of her face, as if to fan away the odor. Then she turned around and walked back to the nurses station. "I can't examine that man until he's had a bath," she exclaimed in disgust.

The nurse at the desk called B. Robert and told him to give the patient a bath in one of the new bathtubs., He wheeled the smelly patient back to his domain, pushed the stretcher behind the screened off area by one tub, and proceeded to undress him and give him the requested bath. This was not without some choice remarks from the patient, which for the purposes of this narrative will remain censored.

Very pleased with himself, B. Robert pushed the stretcher with the now antiseptic-smelling fisherman back to room three, clad in a clean, if drafty, hospital gown and his clothes sealed in a fairly odor-proof plastic bag. "Okay, Dr. Madison, he's all yours."

The young doctor determined our fisherman had pneumonia, serious enough to be admitted.

"His pneumonia is bound to get worse with no more dirt to protect him from real air," B. Robert chuckled when he came back from delivering the fisherman to the medical unit.

When the night shift came to an end, he waited for the day ER supervisor to come. Miss Hornbeck, an ex-Navy nurse, ran the Emergency Department like a tight ship. He was sure she would want to know the events of the night. When she came in, B. Robert went over to her with an obvious sense of accomplishment and told her about the initiation of the new tub.

Miss Hornbeck was suddenly very still. "WHAT?"

His grin turned quizzical. "I just gave the man a bath in the new tub."

"What did you do with all the boxes in the tub?" Miss Hornbeck's expression became stern.

"I stacked them on the floor against the wall. They're still there."

"Young man, the reason the boxes were there was so no one would use the tubs yet. The drains aren't connected. The Pharmacy storeroom is directly underneath."

B. Robert had the good grace to look aghast. "I had no idea."

"Well, can't be helped now. The damage is done. I'll let the pharmacist know what happened. Please put the boxes back into the tub, and this time put a sign on both tubs saying they're not to be used." She heaved a sigh and stalked down the hall muttering about stupid contractors.

He did as ordered, adding, "Drains not connected." To the best of my knowledge, the wonderful new tubs were never used again, although the showers were used later. So much for bells and whistles—great on paper but not always so useful in practice.

A few weeks later, a car drove up behind the ER, and a man and two women in *haute couture* filed into the department, looking a bit shaken but without obvious injuries. Although the evening was not unusually busy, all the rooms were filled and there were a few patients in the waiting room.

"We've had a car accident," the man announced. "Two of the ladies need to be seen at once. We have to get to a reception at the Olympic."

Trina, the nurse on duty, took the names and basic information of the women, and pointed out the waiting room.

"No, no, you don't understand," the man said. "They must be seen at once. We have to be downtown. We're already late."

"We don't have any free rooms, and our doctors are busy seeing patients, sir," Trina said politely but firmly. "Please have a seat, and we'll get you in as soon as possible."

The man drew himself up in all his sartorial splendor. "Do you know who I am? I'm the architect who designed this building."

B. Robert and I were standing at the counter, watching this exchange. With the memory of the bathtubs fresh in his mind, he burst out laughing.

"I wouldn't brag about that!" he said and walked off down the hall.

Trina and I had to smile, even as the architect continued to bluster. Trina told us later that the women had been told they would get red carpet service because of him.

Ah, Progress....

MEDICAL BENEFITS?

The financial status of King County Hospital (KCH) was chronically iffy, and subject to cuts. Employee's health care was provided in-house. There was no money to even partially pay for insurance, so care was offered through the regular clinics, the employee health nurse, and, when necessary, hospitalization. We got free immunizations when needed, and were not charged for any care given at KCH.

Jean, a student who worked only in summer, contracted aseptic meningitis one year. She had taken an early-season swim in Lake Washington, the waters of which were seriously polluted at that time. She was hospitalized on 2-South, the communicable disease ward, and recovered nicely.

Another employee, Abby, developed acute abdominal pain one day while at work and was admitted with a possible bowel obstruction. She was hospitalized for several days in severe pain before the residents determined she was not going to get better without surgery, so reduction of the obstructed bowel was done without complications. (Since bowel obstructions sometimes cleared without surgery, medical treatment was usually tried first.) Abby sang the praises of one of the residents who had stayed with her those first days when she was in so much pain, doing everything he could to ease her misery.

I also had occasions to see a doctor, usually in the ER because of my hours. Once, for a toothache, the intern gave me codeine, which made me remarkably nauseated. Adding insult to injury, he wrote "carious teeth" on my chart. I was miffed—one tooth does not equal *teeth*. Usually, however, my rare visit was for something like bronchitis.

There were other opportunities for medical interactions between employees and the medical staff. The hospital was a research and training arm of the University of Washington Medical School, and employees were sometimes approached for participation in a demonstration or a study. I had the opportunity to participate in one of the former.

The employee health nurse contacted me one afternoon when I came in.

"Dr. Van Arsdale called to see if I could find a volunteer for his medical students in the Allergy Clinic next week, and I thought you might be interested."

Dr. Van Arsdale was one of the clinical professors in the Allergy Clinic. Being a seasonal asthmatic, I had been tested in the clinic and was found to be allergic to the spring and fall crop of pollens and grasses. Being available for the projected time, I agreed to call him back. This promised to be something new and interesting, even if only for one afternoon. "When the clinic begins," he explained, "I will give you a shot of histamine. You'll sit in front of the class of medical students so they can ask you questions and observe your reaction. Don't worry," he smiled. "We won't let anything bad happen to you."

On the appointed day, I trotted up to the Allergy Clinic. As the students filed in, the good doctor drew a small amount of liquid into a syringe from a vial.

"Histamine," he explained to his class, "is a natural substance found in the body, which has a number of functions. The one we are particularly interested in here is the body's reaction when a trigger is encountered. This patient is allergic to pollens and grasses, and although she is not currently having an asthmatic attack, I am going to inject a small amount of histamine to see if we can induce an allergic reaction." Whereupon, he proceeded with the injection.

I gasped. The injection was like liquid fire! He hadn't mentioned that little item. After about five minutes, he had students come up, one by one, and listen to my breathing and take my pulse rate. The students asked me questions about my history and how it usually manifested. I don't recall that my reaction was as acute as he had hoped, but for me, the fire in my arm took much too long to regress. I never volunteered again!

Another employee, Ed, got more than he bargained for by volunteering for a research project. He was an orderly in his late forties, father of nine children, and holding down two full-time jobs in order to make enough money to support his large family. His wife was again pregnant, and this offer came with some extra money, so he leapt at the chance. (We all wondered how he had been home long enough to father yet another child!)

This experiment, Ed told us, was with the Gastroenterology Clinic at the University of Washington Medical School. He was to follow a particular protocol and at specified time periods, a biopsy of his stomach would be done to see what, if any, effect the treatment had on the lining of that organ. (I do not recall what he said about the other details of the study.)

Of course, this study was conducted in the medical school, so the interns and residents were responsible for doing the clinical evaluations and the biopsies, overseen by the medical faculty. The first biopsy went smoothly. The next one produced some bleeding after the biopsy, but not enough for him to lose time from either job. But subsequent biopsies were more traumatic, and after being hospitalized following a later one, he dropped out of the study. The monetary compensation for his participation was not enough to make up for the job time lost. No one had mentioned any possible downside of this experimental protocol, so he had not been prepared for the problems.

When he came back to work, he looked haggard. To add to his miseries, his wife had delivered number ten, who had Down's syndrome. Being a good Catholic, he took that aspect of his life in stride, but did admit relief that his wife had had her tubes tied after delivery.

It is important to note here that in the 1950s and early 1960s, informed consent was not a consideration. The laws establishing informed consent, especially in medical research, were not even on the horizon. Doctors were king: it was their choice what they told patients. The residents were pretty good about giving information—it wasn't often they could play the expert and they relished the chance. But when doing research, usually nothing was said beyond what they were going to do—and rarely included what to expect. After all, they wouldn't want to bias the patient and, thereby the study, would they? Fortunately, laws are now in place that require informed consent, and the serious abuses of medical research are mostly a thing of the past.

For nonmedical staff, questioning a doctor's judgment--even an intern's--was not done. Nurses, too, were cautious about that, especially with attending physicians. It took me a very long time to get beyond that ingrained attitude. Nevertheless, the care we got at King County Hospital then was state of the art, and few complained.

"SNORTIE"

When I first met Helen, she was a registered nurse, floating between evenings and nights in the ER. Blond and blue-eyed, her Norwegian heritage was obvious. Her last name, Snortland, had been shortened to "Snortie" by her friends, and everyone knew her by this nickname. Uniformly good-natured, she helped orient me to the weird and wonderful emergency milieu. By the time I was working nights regularly in admitting, we had become friends.

One night, I went in to register a patient she was working on. He had multiple lacerations, and there were many clamps already on his head. Helen would have liked to have had at least three arms at that moment. The doctor was not in the room, and with both hands busy, she asked me to give her an instrument, indicating one in a sterile tray. Without thinking, I reached my naked hand toward it.

"No, no!" she exclaimed. "Use the forceps! Don't touch it with your hand."

I redirected as instructed, and thought, *there's another reason I don't want to be a nurse. I'd mess up too much.*

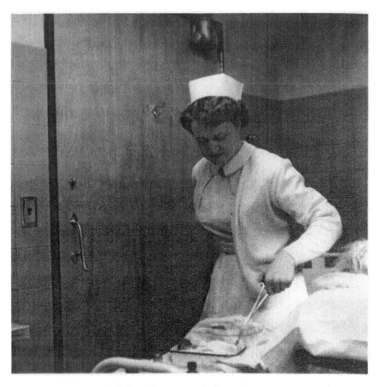

Helen in examining room

Helen had her first experience with what was to become her profession when she was a five-year-old patient with tonsillitis. Two young student nurses pledged to take good care of her when she was admitted for her tonsillectomy. They promised to bring her favorite foods afterward: chicken with mashed potatoes and gravy, and ice cream.

"They did, too," she told me, "but my throat was too sore to eat any of it. They were so nice to me, though, I never forgot it. I think they had a lot to do with my choosing to be a nurse."

Born to a mother from Virginia and an immigrant father from Norway, Helen spent her early years in North Dakota. The family moved to Bellingham, Washington, when she was about nine, where she and her sister grew up through their teen years.

"When my best friend moved to Seattle after we graduated from high school, we got jobs as nurses' aides at King County Hospital right after World War II. We learned everything on the job; there were no training programs then. I did a good job, too. After I got my associate degree in nursing from Everett Community College, I came back to the hospital, and my old supervisor grabbed me immediately and assigned me to ER."

The people working nights were chronically sleep-deprived, so catching a few winks during slack times was common. Helen was no exception. One quiet night in ER, she and two of the interns were in the first examining room, with no patients to be seen. The interns were talking guy talk and Helen fell asleep, bending over with her head on the examining table, but still standing up. They saw her and one said to the other, "Look at that! She's locked her knees and fallen asleep—just like a horse!" She woke up a few minutes later and told him she'd heard what he said.

"No, you didn't. You were sound asleep."

"I know, but I still heard you. Patients can still hear, even if they appear to be sleeping and don't respond."

"It's a good object lesson for them to learn early in their career," she told me later.

The interns marveled at her ability to sleep standing up and the word spread. "You have to see this. Snortie can sleep like a horse!" (Apparently the other lesson was lost on them.) I, too, marveled at her ability: she could also sleep sitting straight up on the counter. Even sound asleep, she never lost her balance

Part of her problem in staying awake was, like many of us, Helen was going to the University of Washington during the day, taking some specialized classes in their nursing program. During that time, she was living near campus, and sometimes invited me for breakfast.

Afterward, we walked over together for classes. I have many fond memories of those mornings.

Once, two detectives well known in the ER were just going off shift as we were, and Helen asked them to join us for breakfast at her apartment. One of them, after walking through her living room, and without turning around, named everything he had seen on entry. Both she and I had to look as he named off things, like papers and their location, the position of a pencil, the color of her furniture, and all the small items on her entry table. We marveled at his accuracy and the amount of detail in his observations. (I called him "Sherlock" after that.)

One of the things not in her job description was monitoring the new interns. She made sure they washed their hands and put on gloves, as well as a lot of little things. It wasn't that they hadn't been taught, but it wasn't second nature to them yet. "We kept them from making a lot of small mistakes—and big ones sometimes."

"But the interns weren't the only ones who didn't have it altogether," she told me. "I was pretty innocent when I started in emergency, too."

One night when the ER was really busy, a man came in and wanted his wife to be seen right away; she'd been bitten by a dog. All the exam rooms were full, so Helen told them to have a seat in the waiting room. The man was really drunk and kind of belligerent and wanted her seen *now*.

"You're just stalling because I'm black," he said, glaring at Helen.

"What's that got to do with anything?" she shot back. "Our rooms are all full—and even your mother would say you're drunk." He backed off then, and just looked at her kind of meekly and sat down.

When at last the woman was taken to an examining room, the man stretched out on a bench and fell asleep. After being taken care of, she came out and asked Helen to call a cab. When it got there, she started to leave, and Helen said, 'Aren't you going to get your husband?'

"Oh, yeah," she said and went back to the waiting room to wake him up. As they went toward the door, she saw the woman stuff a wad of bills down her cleavage.

"I figured she was taking care of his money so he wouldn't lose it; he was still pretty drunk." Helen laughed.

Later that night, while we were having lunch about 2 a.m., a policeman came down to the lunchroom asking questions about the two. Helen guessed at once that the woman was not his wife and that she'd rolled him, which the policeman confirmed.

She told him what she'd seen, and he said she'd have to testify to that in court. As it turned out, the man was a farmer out in the valley and that day had just sold a load of produce and had a lot of money on him. "I can't believe I was that naïve!" She shook her head as she laughed at herself.

Emergency was not the only place in King County Hospital where Helen worked. For a while she pulled duty in the clinics, and also in the operating room. Her passion, though, was working with patients who were awake, not anesthetized. She left before I did, to work as a special duty nurse to individual patients. Of course.

Helen at nursing station

HELP, HELP, POLICE!

Hardly a day passed in the Emergency Department without a visit from the gentlemen of the law—city police, sheriff deputies, warrant officers, even the occasional state patrolman—bringing in or picking up some unfortunate person. The nurses became particularly well acquainted with the regular officers and sometimes liaisons developed, even marriage. One of our day admitting clerks married a policeman, although that didn't turn out too well. After they married he became extremely controlling, not even allowing her to spend time with her friends away from work. (I don't know the ultimate outcome. Everyone lost touch with her once she left the job.)

The personalities of the officers were variable, with slightly different bents. Some were rigidly by-the-book and serious, no jokes, please. But most were "just folks" doing their job, some shy and some outgoing. There were a few we never liked to see coming, those who were abusive to the people they brought in--and sometimes to ER staff. We called them bullies with a badge. One motorcycle cop, with the same name as a well-known comic of the era, thought his coarse misogynistic jokes were hilariously funny. He was so aggressive that his superiors kept pulling him off the street and relegating him to Complaints, away from the public, at least. I had the misfortune to sometimes get him when I called in reports. If I only had one or two cases, I'd put up with talking to him, but if I had more, I called back on another line. He came to a bad end. Someone told me that years later, in a drunken fit, he banged his head so hard against a stone wall that he fractured his skull and died. Fortunately, he was a rarity.

I only remember once having to call the police to help us. One night at about midnight, Trina came flying down the hall to my office.

"Quick, Lynn, call the police! There's a man with a gun at the ER desk. He's trying to shoot a target. He's drunk or on drugs and he won't put the gun away."

I was on the phone before she finished talking. Minutes later we saw the flashing lights of the police car pull up to the entrance. Together, she and I walked cautiously back to the ER desk just in time to see a short, rotund policeman walk through the sliding doors.

"What seems to be going on here?" he said.

The man was still standing at the counter, pointing a pistol at a fat metal figure with a round target in its belly, which he had placed on a small desk against the wall behind the counter. Glassy-eyed, the man took aim at it, but couldn't seem to get his finger situated properly on the trigger.

"I c'n hit it ev'ry time. Jus' watch me."

The policeman quickly reached him and grabbed the pistol. The man looked surprised.

"Don' you wanna see me hit it? I'm really, really good."

"Let's get your little target over there and we'll take it downtown where you can show me how good you are. Guns make these ladies nervous." The policeman motioned for Trina to retrieve the metal object, which she did with alacrity, and he escorted the man to the waiting squad car.

As they drove away, staff and patients appeared out of the woodwork.

A "Whew!" came from almost everyone at once, like air suddenly escaping from a punctured balloon.

Though not high on their list of duties, the police often took patients home when they had no other way of getting there. This happened most often during the late evening and night shifts for obvious reasons. Usually the ER request was met with good grace, but there was one woman who tried everyone's patience, especially the police.

The woman, who had five children, came into the ER regularly, almost once a week during cold weather. One of her children always had an ear infection, a runny nose and cough, or something else minor. Each time the mother was referred to the Pediatric Clinic at the hospital, but she never followed up. Her modus operandi was to arrive late in the evening, the entire family dropped off hastily by someone in a Cadillac. The family lived on the border of the next county, and never arrived with any money. The person who brought them in never returned to pick them up, and the woman always claimed the Cadillac driver had no phone and there was no one who could take them home. Each time, Helen or another ER nurse called the police to come get them. By the time they were seen and ready for discharge, it would be after midnight. The pattern was so predictable that both the police and ER nurses were annoyed. This woman managed to push everyone's buttons.

Most often, the police saw that the family got home. Every once in awhile, on an unusually busy night, the police dispatcher would say, "No, dammit, we're not a taxi service!" But the nurse calling would be insistent, and eventually they would give in. Rides home were far from an every night affair but they happened often enough, given the financial status of our clientele. The police usually took it in stride.

BURN TREATMENT, NATURE'S STYLE

The chronic austerity budget under which King County Hospital operated left little wiggle room for environmental niceties like air conditioning and window screens. On hot summer nights everyone complained and opened the nearest window to get a bit of air movement. This occasionally had unintended consequences.

On one of those sweltering nights, I was catching up on some paper work when Nancy, who was working on the postoperative ward, called me.

"Lynn, when you get a chance, you've got to come up here and see something."

Business was slack at that moment, so I trotted up to Nine-Center, where she took me into a small room that housed a patient who had been badly burned in a house fire. The young woman was sleeping, her head turned to the side. Moonlight bathed the white bandages covering the damaged areas of her neck and torso. The unscreened window was open to allow whatever breeze there was to help cool the uncomfortably hot room.

Nancy took out her pocket flashlight and gently lifted up one of the bandages on her neck. It was difficult to see clearly, but there was a collection of white, moving things under the bandage. I looked up, questioning. Nancy motioned me outside the room and quietly closed the door.

"They're maggots laid by flies," she said. "They only eat dead flesh. They'll leave when they get down to live tissue."

Many years later, she told me she had removed them each night before the patient awoke. She put ether on the maggots and lit a match to destroy them. Each morning she described the situation when she gave her report to the on-coming shift. Nothing happened to change anyone's actions, perhaps because the evidence was no longer present. After several days of being ignored, Nancy stopped destroying them, and let them crawl off wherever they chose to go. It took nearly two days to get anyone's attention, and that was only after the little crawlers had traversed two floors. The next one down was obstetrics, the one below that the operating room.

Finally, the fertile flies with their resulting maggots were eliminated, and a greater effort was made to ensure none reached the burned patient.

The surgeons subsequently took the young woman to the operating room for cleaning and removal of the dead tissue from her burns, a procedure known as debridement, but the maggots had already done the job. The maggots proved the least traumatic method for removing burnt tissue, which the young patient later underwent. The debridements were much more painful.

Nancy only told her about the maggot therapy after she had completely recovered and the patient said she had known something was there; she'd felt them moving.

"Thank you for not telling me," she said. "If I had known they were maggots, I probably would have started screaming and wouldn't have been able to stop."

In subsequent years, I have heard patients describe how very painful surgical debridement of burns can be, but the removal of dead (necrotic) skin is necessary to prevent infection.

If flies lay eggs in open wounds, wouldn't there be something in the history of medicine to indicate it had happened before? Indeed there is. Battlefield wounds were often subject to such infestations— and those wounds tended to heal with fewer infections. Among the Maya and other aboriginal tribes, the effect had also been noted. Maggots were deliberately introduced to reduce infections in battlefield wounds during the Civil War in the United States. The discovery and use of antibiotics in World War II stopped the use of such techniques. However, with antibiotic resistance growing at a rate that alarms most infectious disease experts, interest in maggot therapy is on the rise in appropriate situations.[4]

Granted, the idea of even sterile maggots chewing on one's own dead skin isn't pleasant. But if the option were much greater pain and possibly infection in spite of antibiotics, nature's way might be preferable.

DOG BITE

I saw the station wagon drive up, crowded with people and a couple of dogs, the back piled high with belongings. Parking in the ambulance court right behind my office window, a young woman got out of the back seat, her long black hair falling almost to the ground as she reached inside to pull out a small boy. Holding the crying child tightly, she made her way into the Emergency Room. With no immediate work, I went out to the nurses station, ready to check for a chart on the new patient.

Helen reached automatically for a new Emergency Room form. "Well, what happened to this little guy?"

"He was playing with the dog in the back seat and it bit him."

"Where was he bitten?"

Without words, the woman turned the child around, displaying blood-stained shorts in a sensitive area.

Helen swallowed a smile and asked the usual basics: Had he ever been seen here before (the mother shook her head) and then name, birthdate, address. Finding no record for the little boy, I returned from the Medical Record Department with clipboard and a new patient registration form in hand. Helen pointed me toward the waiting room.

The mother was easy to find. I had noted her unusual dress when she first got out of the car. She wore a long, loose, empire-waist, peach-colored satin dress with short sleeves. I was surprised to see it--my only encounter with the style had been in India, where my sister-in-law, Zareen, had worn such dresses at home in Bombay. Outside of the apartment she always wore saris. This young woman looked as if she might be Indian. I introduced myself and told her I needed some information about her little boy.

"Where did you get your bracelets?" The young woman reached over and touched my arm before I could ask my routine questions. She indicated a pair of sovereign-gold bangles in a bamboo design that I wore, one of the wedding gifts from my Indian mother-in-law.

I told her their origin and she nodded. "I could tell. They're good gold—much better than you can get in this country." Her own gold bracelets and earrings, with their delicate, intricately worked designs, glinted in the dim lights of the waiting room as she gently rocked the child.

The little boy's whimpering had stopped and he was looking around the sparsely populated area. A drunk lying on one of the benches snorted suddenly and half woke up, but immediately fell back into his stupor. A woman sitting in a wheelchair wheezing was taken by an aide to an examining room.

Outside an ambulance turned off its siren and the squeal of tires signaled the arrival of another patient. I sighed and got back to business.

The mother had given the child's name as John Paul. I needed to be sure of the right order and that we hadn't missed any information.

She assured me it was correct. "That's our family name. And we really don't have any address. We don't stay in one place long."

The little boy said something to his mother in a language I didn't know. When she replied in the same language, some of the words sounded similar to the Urdu my husband, Nazir, had taught me some years ago. I asked her if it was Urdu, derived from Persian, or perhaps Hindustani.

She smiled. "No, it's Romani, but Romanis originally came from India."

The pieces of the puzzle fell into place just as the aide came to take them to an examining room.

Another ambulance drove up, followed by a police car.

"Come on, Lynn, admit to 2-North." The ER orderly beckoned to me as he pushed a man on a stretcher down the hall, handing me the stat card as I caught up with him.

Back in my office, I called to notify the floor and complete the necessary paper work for the admission, as well as that for the new young patient.

Toward the end of my shift, I went out to the nurses' station to pick up the completed charts, log them in, and separate out those I would have to report to the police agencies. The Health Department might want the dog bite report. I found the young boy's chart. The diagnosis read, "Dog bite, penis and suprapubic area, with minor laceration." A tetanus shot had been given, and a butterfly bandage applied to the laceration. I smiled. One young boy's potential future was assured--for now.

Looking back on it, the encounter with the boy and his mother was highly unusual. Most often, when Roma, also known as gypsies, arrived, the entire family came in with the patient and fanned out on that floor. Frankly, we dreaded their influx. Unfairly or no, office doors were locked if they hadn't been and personal belongings were secured. Small things often disappeared into waiting pockets. The young children were often noisy and uncontrolled by their parents, who almost seemed to enjoy the ruckus being created. I sometimes wondered whether it was a non-violent way of getting back at the *gadze* (non-Roma) for the discrimination to which they were subjected almost uniformly.

The experience with the mother and son gave me pause. It brought home to me that individual differences exist even within such a tight-knit culture, and that each person needed to be judged on his own merit, regardless of any experience with the "group" to which he might belong.

Perhaps, after all, the other experiences were the "abnormal" and this one, in fact, was the norm.

HAPPENINGS

Several things happened in June of 1955. Thing one: B. Robert got a grant from the University of Washington to dig a site at Celilo Falls, an ancient Indian fishing site on the Columbia River, which was about to be inundated when The Dalles dam was completed. He quit the hospital as soon as school was out, and I promised to come down to help with the mundane living chores when possible.

Thing two was the purchase of my first car—a Plymouth that had been used for parking enforcement by the police department. Its first and second gears were extra-powerful. "You could probably go up the side of the Smith Tower in first," the salesman assured me with a grin. He also pointed out the standard police issue searchlight that had been left on the driver's side. "That's bound to be useful," he said. At last I had *wheels*—no more having to wait for buses.

Thing three was I had to find an apartment. My stepmother had given me notice: my brother was coming home from Yale that summer and "there wouldn't be enough room" if I were still there.

On my next day off, I went apartment-hunting and found a place at the south end of the University bridge, on the corner of Eastlake and Fuhrman Avenues. This strange apartment was on the second floor of a former furniture warehouse. The six-sided tower that would be my doorless bedroom graced the corner of the building, which faced the busy intersection. Across the street was the Red Robin

Tavern, perfect for a glass of wine after classes to get relaxed for an early sleep.

The entrance to my new apartment was hidden behind an enclosed stairwell to the third floor. The Dutch door arched to a point, Hobbit-style, which intrigued me when I saw it and was one of the reasons I decided to take the apartment. The only other tenants were one couple on the second floor with me, and one on the third floor. The other three apartments on each floor were empty while they were being remodeled with new bathrooms being added. Currently, two bathrooms at the end of the hall on each floor serviced all the apartments.

The amenities were limited: heat was furnished by a space heater, although I was assured a wall heater was on order and would be installed before cold weather. The kitchen at the far end of the long room was an "efficiency" type—sink, refrigerator and top stove burners all in one unit. One set of cupboards provided the only storage. The rest of the apartment was unfurnished. But because of the remodeling in progress, the price was right. It was June and the weather was warm and the many windows overlooking the street made it bright and cheerful; the entry door was unique and delightful. What more could one ask?

Well, furniture would be nice. A small table and a couple of chairs were gleaned from the family basement. The rest of the décor was eclectic St. Vincent de Paul.

To celebrate, I invited one of the nurses over for lunch, a first for me. Away from the banter of a group, we both felt a little awkward. I resolved the next time I cooked, it would be for a crowd, and I'd do it Indian style, with which I was better acquainted.

Preparations for an Indian meal take time, so it had to wait until school was out. I invited my more adventurous friends among the

ER staff for a traditional Indian meal. It was an elaborate dinner, complete with a variety of condiments. This wonder was enjoyed on the floor, on a sheet spread out to hold all the *thals* (stainless steel platters), and us. I didn't make them eat with their right hand, as we would have in India. This can be awkward for the uninitiated, and leads to messes. (The turmeric in most Indian dishes stains yellow, not okay on clothes.) The menu included *keema*, (ground lamb curry) with lots of veggies, a *biriyani* (rice with browned onions, diced lamb, raisins and spices), a vegetable curry, and a version of *hulwa,* a sweet dessert, this one made with wheat cereal lightly fried in *ghee* (clarified butter), cardamom, raisins, brown sugar, sweet spices, milk and whipped cream. For condiments, we had green mango pickle I had brought from India, mango chutney, several small dishes of yogurt, and almonds. We gorged ourselves, and spent much of the evening lying flat on our backs to allow for unimpeded tummy expansion, topped off with lots of laughter and story-telling—and a few turmeric spots on the sheet.

That summer I made the acquaintance of Cheeni, the only Indian doctor at the hospital. I don't recall how that came about—perhaps it was my name tag he noticed, or perhaps some of the orderlies or nurses made mention of the Indian dinner I had made. We started going out occasionally, although I was cautious, not fully trusting Indian men yet. We went dancing, and he assured me that if he stepped on my foot, he could fix it—he was chief orthopedic resident that year. I quickly found I didn't need to worry about romantic entanglements with him; he talked often about Carol, the love of his life who lived in another part of the country. So I relaxed and enjoyed the dancing and his gentlemanly company. He finally persuaded Carol to come west and marry him, so ending a short, pleasant interlude.

When I had a weekend off, as promised, I went down to Wishram on the Columbia River, and did the usual camp chores of cooking and shopping for supplies for B. Robert. Under his direction, I held the survey rod for excavation measurements, or helped clean off artifacts. At the end of the day we sometimes swam in the river to cool off from the blistering heat. Sunday nights, I headed back to Seattle to get ready for Monday classes and work.

One summer night when we got off swing shift, all the ER nurses, myself, Sam, and another orderly decided to go to the beach. Irene, one of the nurses with a religious bent, asked if there would be any alcohol. She wouldn't come if there were. Trina reassured her there wouldn't be. We changed clothes, and met at Golden Gardens on Puget Sound after midnight.

The night sky sparkled with stars. A full moon beamed down on the water lapping at the edges of warm sand. Gerry, one of the other nurses, brought cheese and crackers, Irene contributed homemade cookies, and we all had thermoses of tea or coffee, or bottles of Coke. Vanessa, one of the newer nurses, had brought her big Stanley thermos full of a "special tea."

"Would you like to try some of my 'tea' in your coffee?" she asked me, and smiled mischievously.

"Why not," I replied, catching her drift and held out my cup. Sure enough, it "enhanced" my drink. She did not share with Irene.

Sam built a small bonfire in one of the fire pits, and we gathered around it, warming ourselves as the night air cooled. We sang, gossiped, and gradually heads drooped and bodies stretched out on the sand. Some dozed, but no one wanted to leave. Irene, more fastidious than the rest of us, was the first to go home.

Heavy-eyed, we watched the first rays of sun sneak over the top of the cliff behind us to light up the eastern shores of the Olympic

Peninsula. It gave me a strange feeling of impropriety, as if I had committed some *faux pas*. Creatures of the night at play should not encroach on the world of day-timers? As if by command, we gathered up our belongings, made the area pristine once more, and dispersed to our respective homes.

To sleep, to work, and to play again.

A LITTLE TUMULT

As the September days grew shorter and leaves turned to yellows and reds, life settled down to a routine. By now I was fulltime on the graveyard shift. A quick breakfast after work, home to pick up books, morning classes, and then a stop at Red Robin for a glass of wine before piling into bed in the early afternoon to sleep. The constant traffic outside became white noise that drowned out the small noises of car doors slamming and people talking on the street. The only thing that awakened me was the loud clanging of the bell when the University Bridge opened for tall boats, fortunately infrequent once school was back in session. Getting up about 9:30 PM was enough time to prepare a night lunch, and then have a cup of coffee and a bite to eat before going off to work.

Sam and I started having occasional breakfasts and going to the university together. This gradually increased to opening up a nearby tavern together when we got off work some Saturday mornings. He was easy to talk with, and we were comfortable together. I began to hope this would turn into something more serious. My relationship with B. Robert had morphed into a simple friendship, and I liked having Sam in my life.

Sometimes Paul, a night dispatcher in the sheriff's office and my most frequent contact for reporting county accidents, would come by my apartment and join me for coffee about 10 PM. Paul was my buddy. In our initial telephone encounter, when I spelled my name as the reporting clerk he pronounced it correctly the first time. I was impressed, even after he explained that his aunt had been a missionary in India for many years. He and his wife lived up on Capitol Hill a short distance away from my apartment.

One night, the constant swish-swish of cars on the wet pavement below gradually infiltrated my sleepy brain, signaling the time to awaken and get ready for work. The faint illumination from streetlights through the slotted windows in my hexagonally-shaped bedroom barely penetrated my eyelids. Just a few more minutes…

Then the side of the bed sagged under the weight of…someone. My eyes flew open. I felt a hand on my back and my heart stopped for several beats. I didn't breathe.

A familiar voice said, "Hey, Lynn, time to get up and make some coffee."

I breathed again. "Christ, Paul, you scared me to death! How did you get in?"

"The door wasn't locked. You really shouldn't leave it unlocked, you know."

"I didn't. I locked it before I went to bed. Now shoo, and let me get dressed."

Paul went into the living room and turned on a light while I grabbed my robe and work clothes, and trotted to the community bathroom down the hall.

"You'd better get the landlord to fix that lock," he said. "The next person might not be somebody you know."

"He's already fixed it once, but obviously it's still not holding right," I said. "I'll have to bug him again, I guess."

I made coffee, and after a bit of small talk, we went our separate ways.

Later that month, I was getting ready for work at around 9:30 PM when I noticed flashing lights on the street below. A police car roared up beside the line of parked cars next to our building. The siren was off, but the lights drew the attention of customers at the Red Robin, who peered out at the activity. As I watched, two officers leapt out of the car and ran around the corner onto Eastlake, guns drawn. *What unlucky person are they after,* I wondered. Then I heard feet pounding up the stairs from the first floor. *Oh, oh, someone in this building?*

Then banging on *my* door? It had to be someone I knew—I was as innocent of wrong-doing as a newborn babe.

"Open up! Police!"

I flew to the door, opening the top half, and there, grinning from ear-to-ear, were Paul and his captain from the sheriff's department.

"Gotcha!"

"Jeez, you guys, you're going to get me in trouble with everybody!" I opened the door and let them in.

Guns holstered, they plopped themselves into chairs, having a good laugh at my expense. I poured coffee for them, and then pointed out it might be a good idea for one of them to park the car and turn off the lights before someone stole it. The captain dispatched Paul to do the job.

"Cap," I said to the big gray-haired man grinning at me, "haven't you anything better to do than scare the bejesus out of innocent civilians?"

"Just wanted to make sure you were awake. Paul said he had to wake you up the other day."

"Yeah, and scared me half out of my skin in the process."

When Paul came back after parking the patrol car, he asked if I'd gotten the lock fixed. I shook my head.

"They keep trying to fix that old lock and won't replace it. Good thing I don't have anything worth much in here. Of course, nobody sees the apartment since it's behind the stairwell." I didn't mention the couple of drunks that had staggered past the entrance to the stairs trying to reach their friends on the third floor.

I had gotten to know the captain through Paul, and he clearly liked to play practical jokes. Tall, once built like a football player, he had become a bit paunchy, but still believed himself to be quite a catch despite his age, which I guessed to be around fifty—at least. I don't believe he was married. Coffee cup in hand, he told me a wild tale about an orgy which involved Spanish fly. I had no idea what that was, but assumed it must be an aphrodisiac. Behind him, Paul shook his head while the captain told this story, which gave me some doubts about its veracity. When I later asked Nancy about Spanish fly, she told me it was a dangerous sexual stimulant and a potent cause of gastrointestinal and urinary hemorrhage. In the unregulated dosages found on the black market, it could be a killer.

I continued to talk with Paul when I reported to the Sheriff's Department, and he kept me abreast of his growing family. But I never ran into the captain again.

In November, I had an unnerving incident that necessitated another move. With no renters on the third floor now and only one besides me on the second floor, the remodel was moving along rapidly. With my unusual hours, I basically had the bathroom at the end of the hall to myself. Unfortunately, it was unheated. My habit was to run extremely hot water in the tub and wait five to ten minutes to warm up the room, by which time the water had cooled enough to get in. On this night I followed my usual pattern and was just soaping up when I heard an ominous cracking sound overhead. I looked up to see the ceiling bulging and leapt to the front of the tub as the plaster gave way and came crashing down into it. The landlord and I had had a number of differences of opinion about basic amenities, and this was the last straw. I found another apartment ASAP.

A few days later, a cousin helped me move my meager belongings into a new place on Brooklyn and NE 47th (much closer to the university), which boasted one bedroom as well as a living-dining room, miniscule kitchen—and its own little bathroom, and there was heat!

After a thank-you dinner with my cousin, I went back to my apartment and lay down for a nap before going to work. The big bed was so comfortable and the room so toasty warm that I fell asleep immediately. As expected, it was dark when I woke up, and I turned on the light to get ready for work. Glancing at the clock, I discovered to my horror that it was past two in the morning! I had overslept by four hours. Of course, I had no phone so no one could have called me, nor could I call them. I raced to get dressed and flew to the hospital.

When I arrived, Miss Kellogg was in the admitting office. She lived in Harborview Hall across the street, so did not have far to go when the nursing supervisor called her to find out who was supposed to be working. She was very glad to see me, although it was mixed with understandable annoyance at my tardiness. She harrumphed a bit but when I explained, but just said, "Well, thank heavens you're here, at least."

My paycheck was a bit shorter that time.

MISERY

When one is both a student and full-time night-shifter, the never-getting-enough-sleep syndrome can be double trouble. The quarter's end saw most working students living on coffee and amphetamines. I wasn't any different. Toward the end of fall quarter in 1955, I went to work even though I felt ill. After getting off work in the morning, my days were spent in class and at the library.

One week before final exams, all students in Dr. Marts' Water Resources class had to do a paper and present it. It was a small class, only about six of us. Four of the students were seniors, ones I recognized as Geography's "Brain Trust"—a group of brilliant guys who had all taken geology courses, achieving A grades much to the disgust of the professor. Forced to grade on the curve by university policy, the geology professor had had to give lesser grades to his own majors. He was not happy about this and as a result did not like seeing geography majors in any of his classes. (Indeed, when I later took geomorphology from the same man, I worked my tail off just for a C.) I knew, especially as a lowly junior, I had to do something outstanding to keep up with the rest of the students in Dr. Marts' class. I was behind and feeling the pressure. In addition, speaking in public—even to such a small group—terrified me.

By the day of my presentation, I had been up for nearly seventy-two hours straight. I was mildly nauseated, had no appetite, and my right side hurt just from carrying my books. As I sat through presentations by the other students, the only thing keeping me going was the adrenalin brought on by my fear of standing up in front of the "Brain Trust." Somehow, I got through it. To this day I don't remember what I said after the first few minutes. Unlike some other students, I had no handouts, nor did I have the overhead transparencies another had. However, I put a few diagrams on the board, which may have earned me some brownie points. When the bell rang and we turned in our papers, all I wanted to do was crash.

With all the tension gone, the pain in my right side suddenly exploded into my consciousness. So instead of heading for home, I went to the student infirmary and explained my miseries. The doctor took a look at my eyes and pushed hard on the right side of my abdomen, which nearly sent me into orbit.

Dark urine? Clay-colored stools?

Yes and yes.

He called for the lab technician who drew blood, and then, without waiting for the results, said, "I think we need to keep you for awhile. You have infectious hepatitis." (Infectious or viral hepatitis was the old term for hepatitis A.)

Without further ado, I was assigned a room and put to bed. Blessed bed! At last I could sleep. Actually having a disease meant I didn't have to work for at least a few days. But just as I was getting comfortable, I remembered I had to call in and let my boss know. Then I called Sam, and asked him to call my father. That done, I let myself drift off to ZZZZ-land.

Sometime during the evening, my father and stepmother came. I heard the nurse caution them, "Don't stay too long. We've had a difficult time trying to rouse her."

Yeah, I thought, *I'll bet. All I need to do is catch up on sleep.*

The visit was short. I kept falling asleep, and they left after a little bit. Later I learned the nurses were afraid I was on the edge of hepatic coma. Another student, working in a biology lab, had been sent to King County Hospital just a week or two previously, having come in with hepatitis and gone into a coma at the infirmary. But that was not my issue—just sleep deprivation, and, oh, yes, a little hepatitis, too.

The next afternoon Sam stopped by to see me. By then I was a little more functional and asked him to get in touch with my professors and let them know I might miss final exams. He promised to do that.

This was my first time being on the other side of hospital bed sheets. Now I was the patient, subject to the commands/demands of the doctors and nurses. And of course, once I had slept myself out, I wanted to know everything. By the fourth or fifth day, my need for sleep was decreasing, and I found myself wide awake on the night shift—my shift. I took to padding out in my hospital slippers and peppering the nurses with questions.

Why did the doctor admit me without waiting for the lab results?

"Have you looked at yourself in the mirror?" The nurse laughed. "Your eyes are the loveliest shade of yellow. Besides, when your lab tests did come back, they were all so positive, there wasn't any doubt."

Why was I getting so much apricot juice? They were giving me twelve-ounce glasses mid morning and afternoon, so when the next meal came, I had absolutely no appetite.

"To give your liver a rest, you need a high carbohydrate, low fat, low protein diet until your liver enzymes come back to normal."

They were religious about tracking those enzymes. Every morning a lab technician, sometimes two, showed up to draw my blood. Clearly, I was the guinea pig for at least a few students, and my arms began to feel like pin cushions. An older woman, who incongruously identified herself as the chief lab technician, always had difficulty finding a vein. Either it slid away from the needle or it wasn't where it should be or she went right through it—always some excuse. This female sadist wiggled the needle around, trying to find my elusive vein. (I still have a scar or two from her efforts.) Mercifully, the lab techs would call a medical student if they couldn't find a vein after two tries. The medical students who came were swift and accurate on the first try, which made me wonder about the differences in training.

I shared a bathroom with a young student in an adjacent room. One day I asked what she was being treated for.

"I've got a cyst on my butt," she said, grimacing. "They've had to lance it several times. The infection doesn't seem to clear."

Why would they have two hazardous people share the same bathroom? She with an open wound on her sitting apparatus, and I with a disease spread by body fluids! Had anyone considered that? The nurses shrugged when I mentioned it, and just warned me to be careful in my hygiene. Really!

During the midnight hours, I persuaded the nurses to let me call KCH and talk to the evening admitting clerk, Pat, who had been recruited to cover nights while I was gone. This had upset her biorhythms, as well as family rhythms which were geared to her regular evening shift.

"Please, please, get well and come back soon," she pleaded.

By day ten, I was feeling quite good and wanted to go home and get back to normal routines.

"Not yet," the doctor told me. "You need to be eating better and your lab work still isn't close enough to normal."

"Well," I grumbled, "If you'd stop making me drink all that apricot juice, I'd have more appetite." It seemed quite simple to me, and finally he agreed I might have a point. He wrote a stop order, and soon I could actually finish my meals.

By now it was mid December. Final exams had gone by, and I was in my thirteenth day in the infirmary. I'd had enough. The doctor was still reluctant to let me go, but when he said he wanted to wait a few more days, I said no, and signed out against medical advice. Power to the patients!

Finally dressing in my own clothes, the results of so much apricot juice became uncomfortably apparent: I couldn't button my skirt. I had gained ten pounds in those thirteen days. With a rubber band, I managed to assure my skirt would stay on until I got home.

The trek from the infirmary to my little basement apartment several blocks off campus seemed uncommonly long, and my school books heavier than usual. Snow had fallen and the air was fresh and crisp. The world smelled so good after the antiseptic odors of my confinement that I didn't mind being tired in such a short distance. I dropped my books on the table, grabbed a beer from my tiny fridge, and just as I was about to open it, thought—beer—alcohol—liver. No one had said anything, but should I be doing this? I put in a call to the infirmary, and got the doctor on duty.

"No!" she said. "No alcohol for at least six months."

So much for the holidays. Ah, well.

Two days later, I went back to work, much to Pat's relief.

At a New Year's Eve party held by one of the nurses that year, I was the only non-drinker in the crowd. I'm sure I bored them to tears with my complaints about that, but we all celebrated at midnight— even me with my hot apple cider.

How good to be back in my own routine, among all those sick people and my work family.

Lynn and Pat in admitting office of new wing

LETTER TO SAM

February 25, 1956

Dear Sam,

All the experts say it is not good policy to date fellow employees. I thought we were going to prove them wrong, but they were right after all.

It happened so gradually, working so long and so well together as we did. Being able to chat with you in the office when things were quiet gave me a chance to see what kind of person you are. I found a great deal to like, especially your generosity of spirit, your willingness to accept people the way they are, rather than trying to remake them in some other image. Coming recently from a marriage and another alliance in which put-downs were coming at me so often, you were a breath of fresh air, and even something of a refuge. When we disagreed, you could present your views in a calm, nonjudgmental way and never made me feel I was mentally deficient because my opinion was different. Is that, perhaps, why you chose the social work as your goal? You certainly are comfortable to be with, and maybe it's instinct with you to put people at their ease. Even now, after our break-up, I'm not ill at ease working with you, and I thank you for such understanding. Both of us have to work.

We had good times together, though, Sam, and I'll not forget them. The breakfasts after work on our way to classes, and the occasional tavern adventures when we didn't have class. Walks along the Ship Canal or around campus between classes, and the occasional long sleep in my little dark apartment after classes.

Thank you, too, for calling my family the day I wound up in the UW Infirmary with hepatitis, and for letting my professors know I couldn't finish out the quarter. I don't think I ever told you how much I appreciated that. You saved my academic hide.

Your devotion to your family was always evident, and I respect that. I had no quarrel, either, with your religious viewpoint, even though I didn't share it. Had you come at me with missionary zeal, like one of the others did, I would have backed away from you right from the start. But you honored my more agnostic views, and even agreed with me about the church's man-made politics, citing your father's Baptist ministry as an example.

I guess those are reasons why it was such a surprise blow when you took me aside just as I was coming on duty, and told me we were going nowhere and you wanted out. But you gave away the real reason when you mentioned your father, the Baptist minister, could not give approval to his son's serious involvement with a divorced woman, especially one outside his racial background. After I'd had time to think about it—and believe me, that night at work was an ordeal—I could allow myself to believe your rejection wasn't entirely because I was such an uninteresting person, but rather because your father forced the issue. And you have always been a good son.

So I wish you well, Sam, once you start fulltime in the graduate school at UW. We will all miss you at work when fall quarter begins. Nancy wants me to meet a friend of hers whose girlfriend ran off with another man a while back—with rascality aforethought, I'm sure, to help me get over you. It might work—but you're a hard act to follow.

Warmest regards,

Lynn

POSTSCRIPT

On a blustery March night, Nancy invited me to dinner at her apartment to meet her friend Bob Regudon. Two jilted people in need of renewal. Over fried chicken as only Nancy could make it, we sized each other up.

He was a carpenter, a Navy veteran who came from a large family with a Filipino father and white mother. His features and coloring were distinctly from his father, but his medium height and stocky build clearly came from his mother's side of the family.

An avid reader, some of his choices impressed me: Ayn Rand's *The Fountainhead,* Emil Ludwig's *The Nile*, both of which I had among my own books. He had had one quarter at the University of Washington but quit to go into the Navy, and needed to work once he got out. Well-mannered and articulate, he was clearly intelligent despite his lack of a formal college education.

At the end of the evening, we made a date to see each other again. Nancy was ever so pleased at the outcome of her attempt to play cupid—and even more so when she walked down the aisle of the Unitarian Church as my matron of honor at our wedding that August.

WORK AND THE BRILLIANT PEASANTS

With all the new space, the Medical Records Department work force expanded, and it became a 24-7 operation. The clinics had also expanded, which meant more charts to be pulled daily. There was still only one ER admitting clerk on each shift, but at least there was another person on graveyard shift to pull charts for the ER. And now there was also an evening supervisor in Medical Records. With all the records in one place, the decision to rearrange the filing system was made, changing it from straight numerical to a newer terminal digit system, which theoretically made misfiling harder to do and the misfiles that did happen easier to find. The period during which this revision took place was something of a nightmare, and I suspect some lost charts were never found—but that's just a suspicion. Fastidious Harriet in the storage file room oversaw the new file room in the basement, and if she didn't develop an ulcer during the change-over, it would have been a miracle.

The evening and weekend shifts saw an expansion of the number of employees who were students in their weekday lives. There was tall, skinny, red-haired Jan, who, like many of us, attended the University of Washington. Jean, short, blond, and bursting with energy, came to us on summer breaks from a different university. Then there was

Dan, husband and father of a number of children, who worked thirty-two hours on the weekends and attended law school during the week.

Among the orderlies, there was also B. Robert in anthropology; Sam, who was finishing his undergraduate degree and headed for graduate school in social work; a husband and wife team already in graduate school; another orderly planning on law school; as well as several others whose majors I have forgotten.

The 1950s was a time when even the low salaries for clerks and orderlies allowed for the college tuition and books without running up lifetime debts. The availability of night classes was meager, and the ones that existed were geared to leisure-time subjects. It was not surprising then that night employees at the hospital often were part- or full-time students in their day-time life.

A great deal of underutilized brain power existed among the evening and night staff, and over-qualification in a job sometimes gives rise to the search for other challenges—or mischief.

To the best of my knowledge, I was the only one in our department to take advantage of the patient records for a university course. For my cartography class, I proposed plotting the locations in the city where patients who had attempted suicide lived, looking for any patterns. No addresses were identified, only the area of the city from which the patient came. My instructor agreed and I presented my idea to Miss Kellogg, who approved it.

"You'll have to pull the charts and refile them when you're finished. And you understand it has to be done on your own time outside of work hours," she said.

The woman who maintained the disease index[5] checked the proper codes and I extracted a list of one hundred charts. Over the next few days after work, I pulled them. Assembling the data didn't take long, but drawing the map itself to the rigorous cartographic requirements took quite a bit longer.

Not long after that, Miss Kellogg retired and a new department director was hired. Mrs. Drake was in her late forties and a new graduate of the Providence School for Medical Record Librarians, as the profession was then called. A sturdy woman of average height, blond, with large blue eyes behind thick glasses, she won over her new employees with her friendliness and hearty laugh. Her door was always open, and she was a hard worker. When the day shift had gone home, Mrs. Drake was usually still in her office, often until 9 or 10 PM. This afforded those who worked afternoons the unusual opportunity to get to know our boss on a more personal level. I quickly grew to like her.

"She works much too hard," one of our student contingent commented one night at dinner. "I wonder if there's something we could do to help her."

"Why don't we meet with her," another suggested. "We can see if there is anything she does that we could either take over or help with."

The plot thickened. We were aware the day clerks were periodically annoyed with us. They accused us of leaving too much work for them. It did happen, of course, but only when we were swamped--sometimes by the work *they* left *us*. These are normal bits of fussing whenever a department is open 24-7, but there had been a recent up-tick in complaints. This factored into our plan.

"Let's leave Mrs. Drake a note that says the evening and night-shift staff would like to meet with her next week," one suggested. I was scheduled to be working night shift in admitting the following week, and agreed to come in early. The day was decided upon and Jan wrote the note, leaving it on our boss's desk the Friday before. As best I can remember, it read: "Dear Mrs. Drake, we would like to meet with you on Wednesday at 3 PM to discuss some issues." It was simply signed, "The evening and night staff."

We knew the day-timers would find out and wonder, and rubbed our hands with glee at the thought. We didn't stop to consider how the terse note might affect Mrs. Drake.

Before starting my shift on Monday night, I had coffee with Pat, the evening admitting clerk.

"Medical Records is all a-twitter," she chuckled. "Some of them are convinced the whole shift is going to quit."

"Really! They can be kind of bitchy, but not enough to make us do that. Besides, who could afford it?"

"I think some of them have made Mrs. Drake concerned. Maybe you should have told her why you wanted to meet, so she wouldn't be worried." Pat was in on the scheme, but had chosen not to be part of it because of the unpredictability of ER activity.

Wednesday afternoon we five conspirators gathered just outside Medical Records. As we went in, we noticed everyone's eyes turned in our direction, and then quickly turned back to their work. We walked together down the gauntlet of desks in front of the window, to Mrs. Drake's office at the other end of the room. She looked tense, and motioned us in. When she closed her door, we could almost see the ears moving in our direction.

Mrs. Drake took a deep breath as she sat down. She turned a ring around and around on one finger, folded and unfolded her hands, finally clasping them together on her desk.

"Well, ladies, what did you want to see me about?" she said.

We hadn't planned who was to do the talking, so after a pause, Jean, the summer relief clerk, began.

"We've seen how hard you work, Mrs. Drake, and how late you are here so much of the time. We wanted to see if there was anything we could do to help you out--something we might help with or take off your hands altogether."

"There are times on nights in admitting," I piped up, "when there's very little business and not much to do. Is there something I can do when things are quiet?"

That good lady, now convinced we were not there to lodge some dire complaint, let out a long breath. Taut muscles loosened, she leaned back and laughed.

"That wasn't exactly what I was expecting. If you had let me know what you wanted, I might have an immediate answer for you, but I need to give it some thought. Let me get back to you in a day or two."

And get back to us, she did. I took over the census verification and the monthly payroll, both of which fit nicely into what I did already. At night I used the census daily to make up the discharge lists, so doing the extra checking took very little time. Payroll went in one week before the end of the month, and I could enter data, a little bit at a time, so it was ready for her to check over before she sent it in.

Gradually, her night-time presence decreased until it was a normal 8 AM to 5 PM. I cannot honestly say it was all due to us, her brilliant peasants, and the extras we took over. She grew into her job, too, and developed better time-management skills and learned more about delegating. Only many years later, as a medical records manager myself, did I realize how badly we had handled that encounter, even if our hearts were in the right place.

CALL AN AMBULANCE!

"Hey, Gus, long time no see. Where've you been?" Leaning over the counter at the nursing station, I looked at the tall, skinny driver who was getting ready to return his now-empty stretcher to the ambulance. His cousin, Martin, owned the ambulance company he worked for, and we hadn't seen Gus for about six weeks.

"Been in the hospital," he replied, parking his stretcher along the outside corridor wall.

"What happened?"

"I was in an accident. Totaled one of the ambulances."

"Good grief! Bet Marty didn't like that."

"Yeah, he was pretty pissed."

"C'mon, Gus, spill it. Give with the sordid details." I poked him in the shoulder.

Grinning, he leaned on the counter and told us the whole story.

One afternoon, Gus was on his way back to their headquarters after delivering a patient to a nursing home. He was alone in the ambulance and noticed a car following him a little too closely for comfort. He pulled over to let the car pass, but it didn't, instead pulling in behind him. Gus moved back out on the road and accelerated. So did the car.

At a stoplight he took another look at the car and noticed the driver was a woman. When the light turned green, he peeled out, hoping to lose her. She sped up right behind him again. He made a turn onto a side street; she followed. He made several other turns, but the woman stuck like glue. Exasperated, he headed back to a main road in the south industrial district, and poured on the gas. She followed, tight on his rear. Then he slammed on the brakes.

Both drivers were hospitalized, Gus with a fractured leg and multiple lacerations.

"Of course, I got a ticket for speeding, but she got the big one for following too close. When the cop asked me why I hit the brakes, I told him I saw a squirrel run into the street." Gus was all innocence.

"Never occurred to you to stop and ask her why she was following you?" interjected a nurse who had been listening.

"Nah. Just wanted to lose her. She pissed me off."

"She must have been hurt pretty badly, too. What happened to her?"

"I dunno. They took her to a different hospital."

"How'd you find out they gave her a ticket?"

"The cop came to the hospital to find out what happened and gave me the ticket there. He told me about the ticket she got. I didn't ask him about her. Probably should have."

"Jeez, Gus." I shook my head. "You're some piece of work." I didn't tell him what kind.

Like ham and eggs, ambulances and emergency rooms go together. With or without sirens, these conveyors of misery arrive frequently on any given day of the week, disgorging their passengers for care or transfer at the behest of a physician. The drivers and the attendants become well known to the ER staff.

The medical training then was nothing like the rigorous educational background required currently for emergency medical technicians and paramedics. A good driving record with a cab driver's knowledge of the city and its environs, and basic first aid were, to my observation, the major requirements during the 1950s and early 1960s. Ambulances did not carry much in the way of medical equipment other than oxygen, a stretcher, and linens. None of the drivers or ambulance attendants were women, and I personally do not remember any minorities among their number. Indeed, Nancy remembered there were a few we referred to as "rednecks." In most cases they kept their prejudices to themselves and treated patients of all shades with respect, at least in their presence. The few who noisily did not, found themselves looking for a different job--like the pair who trashed an elderly black patient's apartment when they picked him up.

The uniforms and ability to use the sirens as they chose gave some of them a sense of power. They had their mischievous moments, turning on the siren and racing to their favorite restaurant for a meal—reprimanded, if caught. Others were would-be race car drivers, eager to turn on the siren so they could legally careen down the streets, weaving in and out of traffic.

Most of them, drivers and attendants alike, stuck to their jobs-- trying to get patients to the hospital in no worse condition than when they were picked up. That wasn't always possible, but at least they tried.

The ambulance crews were a necessary part of the ER. Some we liked, others not so much. Gus was among several who were kind of borderline in our view. They didn't seem to use the best judgment, but were basically friendly. Then there were the ones who made crass jokes about sex and/or women or bad-mouthed patients for any reason. Fortunately, those were a small percentage of the ambulance personnel we dealt with. Although they did not have the high level of training and the professionalism of the current EMTs and paramedics, they were still part of our ER family, warts and all.

GERTRUDE

Gertrude started as a file clerk in the Medical Record Department at the age of about eighteen. Somehow, I never think of anyone named Gertrude as being under forty, much less just out of high school. But this one was, and she looked very unlike my idea of a person with that name. She quickly asked us to call her Trudy, which we all agreed fit much better.

She had shoulder-length, wheat-colored hair that turned up slightly at the ends. Her eyes were big and blue with long, thick lashes. Her skin was a cafe-au-lait color (lots of "*lait*") that took on a deep tan in the summer sun, and her mouth a perfect bow with color that needed no lipstick. Combined with a well-endowed shape, she was quite a head-turner.

Despite our initial suspicions about pretty girls' work ethic, Trudy won us all over. On the job, she put in a solid eight hours instead of finding ways to slack off. Once she knew the medical record procedures, she was trained to relieve in the admitting office. She was a quick study, interested in everything, and, joy of joys, good-natured. The ER staff and the patients took to her immediately. She had a delightful, tinkly laugh that made anyone who heard it chuckle right along with her, and her smile lit up the whole department. She was completely natural.

Trudy and I hit it off right from the start, so when she volunteered for night shift, I was delighted. Both of us were relatively easy-going, and liked the camaraderie with the emergency room staff. We had the same work habits—we liked to do the job right and thoroughly. Though we each rotated shifts on occasion, when we worked together, our offices ran like well-oiled machines. If the emergency room got too busy, Trudy would come over and help out without being asked.

It was on the evening and night shifts that we really got to know the ambulance drivers and police officers who brought in many of the patients. There was much good-natured razzing back and forth, especially between the ambulance drivers and the staff. If the drivers had no calls, sometimes they went to the cafeteria for coffee and a snack. They frequently asked Trudy to go with them and when she could, she would. Trudy attracted the ambulance drivers like iron filings to a magnet. We warned her they were a lecherous bunch, but when they said they just wanted to be friends, she believed them. I thought she was much too trusting.

One Saturday night when Trudy was off duty, four of the drivers from an ambulance company close to the hospital invited her over to their company's on-call lounge. The lounge was a common room for the live-ins and the drivers between calls.

Sunday night Trudy came to work shaking her head. When I asked her if something had happened, she chuckled.

"Hank asked me over to their place Saturday night for a little party."

"How was it?" I asked.

"Kind of boring. All they wanted to do was drink. I went along with it for awhile, but they got so drunk, I just left and went home."

The next time Hank came in with a patient, I drew him aside. "Okay, spill it. What went on Saturday night?"

He smiled ruefully. "Boy, I don't know where she puts it, but that kid drank us all under the table. We had hangovers that wouldn't quit! We could barely stand, and she walked out without missing a step."

"Serves you right! What were you thinking?" I looked at him suspiciously.

"We just thought we'd see what she was like when she loosened up." He seemed a bit too defensive.

"Yeah, I just bet. She isn't even twenty-one, you know."

Hank and the other drivers developed a sheepish admiration for Trudy. She just wanted to be friends, and they reluctantly let it go at that. However, things changed when a new attendant, Jimmy, was hired.

Jimmy was blond, blue-eyed and painfully shy. He actually blushed when he first met Trudy one night in the ER. Some spark must have passed between them. They gradually became an item, and one day Trudy came in, head so far in the clouds that her feet barely touched ground. "Jimmy asked me to marry him." She glowed, and so did Jimmy. He even forgot to blush when I congratulated him.

Summer graduated into fall and early winter. The rains came but could not dampen the affection Trudy and Jimmy had for each other. They began to talk about setting a wedding date. It seemed a perfect match.

About ten o'clock one cold and rainy November night, the on-duty nurse got a call from the dispatcher that three ambulances were on the way, one with a patient and two with the crew from an ambulance, which had overturned on the way to pick him up. The patient's home was down a dark, winding gravel road in a rural area. The ambulance driver had been going too fast, skidded around a corner, and lost control. This was before seat belts, so the attendants and the driver had been flung around inside the vehicle as it careened off the road.

One had actually been thrown out as it rolled several times down a steep bank.

The first ambulance arrived with the original patient. After they had put him into a treatment room, the ambulance driver, Hank, came back to my office.

"Is Trudy on tonight?" When I nodded, he shook his head grimly. "Don't let her near the ambulances that are bringing in the crew. You heard about it, I suppose. They won't be bringing Jimmy out of the ambulance."

Trudy knew that Jimmy was one of those coming in because she had gone to pull the medical records for the emergency patients. After pulling the charts, she came back to my office to wait--my windows overlooked the ambulance court. Hank stood up to leave as she came in, but Trudy cornered him and demanded to know what had happened. He told her what he knew about the accident.

Then she asked the question he had been dreading. "How is Jimmy? Is he badly hurt?"

"Trudy, he's... pretty badly injured. He was thrown out and the ambulance rolled over him." Hank could not bring himself to tell her what he knew, but I gave him credit for trying to prepare her for the worst.

Trudy paled and was silent. The second and third ambulances drove in, and she ran to the entrance. Hank and I quickly followed. Joe, the ambulance driver from Jimmy's crew, walked in with only a bump on his head. Charley, the other attendant, was brought in groaning on a back board and wearing a cervical collar. He was bleeding from a head wound and had several lacerations on his face. He was quickly pushed into the critical care room. Trudy waited. The third ambulance parked and the driver closed the vehicle's door and came into the ER, not meeting Trudy's eyes.

"We need a doc in the ambulance," he said to the nurse behind the counter.

Trudy was still, her face white. She was well aware what that request meant: The person in the ambulance was presumed D.O.A. She watched the doctor go out, waited while he examined Jimmy, and watched him come back in, the doors closing behind him.

"I have to see him. I have to. This can't happen."

Hank took her arm and moved to stop her, but she wrenched away from him and ran to the ambulance, Hank close behind. He went into the ambulance with her.

By this time everyone in the Emergency Department knew it was Trudy's fiancé who was D.O.A. When she hadn't come out of the ambulance after a few minutes, one of the ER nurses went out to see if she could help. She was able to persuade Trudy to come back inside. Hank trailed behind.

Trudy was glassy-eyed and dazed. "He can't be dead," she said over and over. "There's not a mark on him, just dirt."

I frowned and looked at Hank, who shrugged.

The doctor who had examined Jimmy came out and sat with her. "His neck was broken, Trudy. He probably never felt a thing."

She looked at the doctor for a minute or two, then stood and walked back toward Medical Records without saying a word. I followed.

"Trudy, honey," I said, "Why don't you go on home. I can manage."

"No, I'm okay. I haven't pulled all the clinic charts for tomorrow yet."

"If you change your mind, it's no problem. I can handle it." I tried to put an arm around her. She ducked her head, her eyes filled with unshed tears, and pulled away from me. I felt so bad for her, but being only a few years older, I didn't know how to help ease her grief. I had never lost anyone close to me.

"No, I have to keep busy. I'll be fine."

She finished her shift and left as soon as the first of the day staff arrived. We never saw her cry on the job, but it was a long time before she smiled again. Within the next year, she found a different job, away from the constant reminder of that awful night.

Death is not an uncommon event in a trauma hospital, but rarely is the death so personal to a staff member. You grow up working in an emergency room, like it or not. The continuum of the life cycle is always in evidence, but the beat of the hospital goes on.

THE SAILOR

Once in awhile, a person was brought in for Psychiatry who really did not belong there. One night, two burly policemen brought in a dark-skinned, dark-haired man in a sailor's uniform. He was shouting and struggling. No one could understand a word he said. They had found him downtown in a bar, shouting at the bartender and waving his arms threateningly at the other customers. The bartender had called the police and because he seemed to be incoherent and talking gibberish, they brought him to us. One of the doctors came out to talk to him, and for a moment the man calmed down and said something in a foreign language. When the doctor shook his head and indicated he did not understand, asking the question again, the man started shouting and struggling, pointing at the police and then at the door.

The doctor took a stat card off the desk and wrote, "Possible psychotic break" and handed it to the nurse standing by.

"Psych?" asked one of the officers, and the doctor nodded. They hauled the man down the corridor to the elevator. I called the floor to let them know they were getting a belligerent patient about whom we knew nothing. Would one of them please give me a call once they got him settled if he had any identification on him?

The orderlies were able to get some information after they got him undressed and locked up. He was a sailor off a merchant ship now in port, but his name and the ship's name were about all they could get. Every little bit helped, and his name appeared to be Arabic.

In the early 1950s, the languages for which we could readily get interpreters on the west coast were European and Asian primarily, which comprised our biggest ethnic groups in Seattle. No one here knew much about the Middle Eastern or African languages, so there was no one who could communicate with this man.

The next night, following up on this patient, I found that someone on Psychiatry had called one of the local universities' foreign student office and found someone who knew what language he was speaking. It turned out to be Arabic, and at last an Arabic-speaking student came down to the hospital and was able to get the man's story.

The patient, Mahmud, had left his ship with some other comrades to have dinner and a night on the town while they were in port. Somehow he'd become separated from his companions and had entered the bar, trying to find out how to get back to his ship. When no one understood him, he became angry and kept repeating his questions louder and louder. Then the police arrived, dragging him away to the hospital. He was terrified and started struggling to get away. He had no idea what was happening to him. When he was put inside a locked room, he thought he had been taken to jail and was petrified that he would miss his ship's sailing and would be held in this "jail" in a foreign country for Allah knows how long.

As soon as the interpreter had clarified what was happening, the man's ship was contacted, and one of the ship's officers came to pick him up. The relieved patient apologized for the trouble and the staff members on the floor, via the interpreter, wished him well, in turn apologizing for not having someone there who could speak his language.

I often wondered how he told that story to his family and friends when he got back home.

FOREIGN BODY

The practice of medicine is an inexact art, especially when done by interns and residents. It is fraught with the potential for innocent error--either through ignorance or lack of adequate experience. Although I have rarely heard of deliberate acts of malpractice, there are many instances when impatience or failure to follow established procedures lead to such a result. And it's not always clear until much later when these incidents do happen.

Around 11 PM one evening a man came in with severe abdominal pain. He told the nurse that he had had the discomfort in varying degrees for several years. The pain had begun after he had had surgery for a ruptured appendix—at our hospital about seven years ago. He had seen a number of doctors about his on-going discomfort, mostly in Idaho and Montana, where he had gone to work after the surgery. None had solved the problem.

The nurse called me to get his medical record, and after bringing it I went back to my office. As usual, business picked up around midnight and I forgot about that particular patient, although I did notice him as he went by on his way to X-ray about 1 AM. An hour or so later, he was brought back to me--this time for admission. After I updated his demographic information, I notified the Surgery floor that they had a new patient coming, with a diagnosis of "Foreign body in abdomen." He would be going to the operating room first.

About 4 AM, Emergency had quieted down and I was starting to do some of the night's statistical work, when Tom, the x-ray technician, came around the corner and beckoned to me. "Come here, Lynn, you've got to see this. We got a doozy in tonight."

I followed him over to the X-ray reading area, and he put up a pair of x-rays on the light box. "Remember that guy with the abdominal pain? Well, look at this!"

He pointed to the films and there, big, bold, and white against the black-and-gray background of the negatives was a broken surgical clamp.

"No wonder the poor guy was in pain! It's amazing he didn't have perforated organs everywhere. And guess who did the surgery—Dr. [X] who's now chief of surgery at [another] hospital. He was just a resident when this happened."

I marveled at the sight and winced a bit on learning that the same doctor was now chief surgeon at another hospital. We speculated on how it could have happened--sponge and instrument counts are supposed to be correct before the surgeon closes the incision. We guessed that either the instrument nurse miscounted or the surgical resident, perhaps even the attending surgeon, had become impatient when the count was off more than once and assuming the nurse was wrong had gone ahead and closed the patient's abdomen. Of course, postoperative abdominal pain would be expected--even postoperative infection would be anticipated with a ruptured appendix—so the patient's pain hadn't triggered any concern.

In today's litigious climate, such an error would have made for a malpractice suit. In those days, however, lawyers were not the first thing on the patient's mind when results were less than perfect.

Although the surgical resident was likely initially responsible for this bit of malpractice, what about the other doctors the patient had seen over the intervening years? Had not even one thought to take an abdominal x-ray? It was unbelievable--to us nonphysicians. But the good news was that the problem had been identified by an intern in the Emergency Room following established procedures. It was being solved even as we spoke--by a surgical resident in the operating room.

MARRIAGE AND MINOR MISADVENTURES

Just before our wedding Bob and I moved into a new two-bedroom apartment with much more space. My colleague Jan moved in with us to help offset the higher rent. Frugality was our game plan. The wedding was scheduled for the day after payday.

The ceremony took place at University Unitarian church—an honest-to-gosh church wedding between Bob, a back-slid Catholic, and me, a practicing Pagan. Jan's mother made my wedding dress from a pale-green georgette sari I had brought from India. My orderly friend, Dick, made our weddings rings and a matching pair of earrings for me, a unique, simple design in silver. Nancy was matron of honor, and dressed to the nines she preceded me down the aisle. Bill, Bob's best friend and a fellow carpenter, was best man. The sister of another orderly friend sang, and my bouquet was freshly picked that morning—Queen Anne's lace flowers from a hillside near our apartment. Even the minister had offered to do the nuptials free as a favor to his friend, the retired minister from the People's Center. And, of course, my father gave me away—for free.

Following the ceremony, we held the reception at our place. Of course, a few small things went awry—what wedding would be complete without that? The worst was that the keg of beer we had arranged to keep cool in a nearby cold storage facility had partially frozen and attempts to draw from it produced a great deal of foam but not much liquid.

Friends from the hospital and university augmented our families at the reception. There were even a few who had not come to the wedding itself, including a shy young man from my cartography class who had a few days before called to ask for a date. I gently declined, explaining I was getting married, and invited him to the reception as he knew others from the same class who were coming—and he came. The men hovered in fascination around the foamy beer keg; Jan and I got out the food.

Only the next day did I discover I had forgotten to put out a big plate of ham, but no one missed it. The frozen beer finally thawed and everyone ate, drank, and was generally merry, except for one girl who drank too much and cried a lot. No one seemed to know who she was.

A congratulatory call from B. Robert came with the announcement that he, too, was getting married--to a girl from the Netherlands whom he had met in The Dalles. We would meet Tessa soon, he promised.

The day after the wedding, we left for a sort-of honeymoon, camping in eastern Washington and exploring the Sun Lakes area. At least it was inexpensive—and we had a lot of ham.

A new life had begun.

RETURN TO REALITY

It's strange—when you undergo a major change in life, you have an expectation that somehow every part of your existence will also be different—and it isn't. Coming back to work after a week in the wild, everyone looked the same and gave the usual harried greetings. The office did not glow in gold. The typewriter was still the old electric. No miraculous leap of technology had replaced the ditto machine. So with a sigh, I settled back to reality.

And sure enough, when it came time to run off the admissions and discharges on the ditto machine, it whirled a couple times, spit a spring at me, and stopped. After about fifteen minutes of futilely trying to fit the spring back into place, I realized it was broken. Now what? I asked around and someone suggested I call the engineer's office. Frank, the night engineer, told me to bring the offending part over. There might be a spare part that would work.

I used the passageway beneath Ninth Avenue that ran from the hospital into the nurses' quarters across the street to bring the spring to him. Per his instructions, I followed the high-decibel sound of the boilers and found his office. Poring through a tray of miscellaneous parts, he found a spring that was close in size, and came back to the office with me to install it. That was the beginning of a delightful friendship.

Frank was probably in his early fifties then, a relatively short, stocky man with salt-and-pepper hair, and a twinkle in his eyes. He always dressed in the dark-gray shirt and pants all the engineers wore. We sometimes shared night coffee breaks, and he would recount his experiences in other jobs. But it was his description of a heating/cooling system he had installed in his own home in Seattle that warmed my ecologist's heart. As a geography major, conservation of natural resources was of prime interest to me. Here was a man who had plumbed the depths beneath his house to bring the earth's heat into his home, a wonderfully non-polluting system.

"In midwinter," he told me, "the ground temperature is around fifty-five degrees, and only needs to be heated just a little bit to be comfortable. In the summer, we don't have to do anything but let that nice cool air drift up into the house. The installation isn't cheap but it's saved us a lot over the long haul."

This was well before the current use of heat pumps, and the system was his own creation, inspired from the heating systems in Iceland, where geothermal power was used extensively. His description inspired me to do a paper on the subject for one of my classes.

Frank had his moments of mischief as well. The intercom that sat on my desk became a weapon in his hands. I was never sure how he knew when things were slack in ER during the night shift, but he was unerring. Taking advantage of an absence of patients, I sometimes put my head down on the desk to catch a quick nap. Suddenly the intercom would explode with the roar of machinery, followed by a loud, "NOW HEAR THIS!"

Reflexively pressing the talk button, I responded, "Ok, Frank, I'm awake!"

Then he would laugh and say, "Gotcha!" He did it often enough that it became a joke between us. Apparently, I was his only victim.

During the year of my wedding, a couple of relief orderlies were assigned to ER who left me with indelible memories. One was Michael, young and full of disorganized energy. He tended to be more in the way than helpful. He was generally assigned as a float between the floors and the ER. From Michael there was much talk and little listening. The ER staff complained that their instructions had to be repeated often.

Michael had developed an alcohol habit in high school and in the process of trying to shake his addiction, a local church had grabbed him and Michael had found Religion. As a practicing Pagan, Michael considered me an appropriate target for his missionary zeal. I was not impressed.

"How can you not believe in God?" he would ask earnestly.

Let me count the ways, Michael!

"He will forgive all your sins—we're all sinners, you know."

"No, Michael, I don't know that." At that point, I usually looked for any avenue of escape and took it. When I finally dredged up the ancient history that I was a baptized a Judson Baptist (in my own misbegotten youth), he finally dropped the subject.

Jake was another float occasionally assigned to ER. Unlike Michael, he listened much and talked little. Quiet, with a shock of straight blond hair that kept falling over brilliant blue eyes, he was a young man who did his job well. In demeanor he reminded me of my good friend, Dick. His passion was climbing mountains, and supporting that passion appeared to be the only reason he worked. Though I did not know Jake well, being an armchair mountaineer, I asked him often about his climbing adventures. This was one subject on which he could wax eloquent, and his exploits always fascinated me.

Like Dick, Jake came to occasional ER parties, and though not the chatty type, he was always a part of whatever was going on. He smoked and drank like the rest of us, blending in well with our gang. There was something about Jake that made him special to me—some aura, some quirk of personality, perhaps curiosity about that part of him that he kept to himself.

Then one Sunday night in summer, Michael, the newly minted Christian, bounced into the admitting office the moment I walked through the door.

"I saved Jake's life!"

"Really. How did you do that?" I looked at him skeptically.

"Jake and I went climbing on Mount Si yesterday," Michael replied.

"Have you ever climbed before?" I asked.

"No. That's why I wanted to. Jake said he'd teach me about climbing."

"So, what happened?"

His reply was a long-winded, confusing description of the event, the end result being that Jake had fallen and Michael had "rescued" him. Mount Si, close to Seattle, is not a high mountain but has claimed a few lives over the years. It is a favorite climbing site on weekends and is considered an easy trek that can be accomplished in an afternoon.

I ran into Jake at coffee later that week, and told him what Michael had said. He shook his head.

"Well, he exaggerated a bit, actually. He did something I specifically told him not to do, which pulled me off balance. Mount Si isn't a hard climb, but you have to pay attention."

Then one day Jake was gone, off to Wyoming, someone said. Rumor had it he married and opened a ski store in Jackson Hole, Wyoming--mountain country, where climbing was a way of life. It seemed a logical choice for him.

Some years later, when Dr. Tom Hornbein's book, *Everest, The West Ridge*, was published, Bob and I added the book to our home library. We were intrigued because the 1963 American Expedition to Everest had a strong cohort of Northwest climbers. Of the nineteen, there was Dr. Tom Hornbein, anesthesiologist, then on leave from the Navy, later a University of Washington Medical School professor; Jim Whitaker and Barry Prather from Washington; William Unsoeld and Luther Jerstad from Oregon; Barry Corbet from Jackson Hole and his business partner—Jake!

But my excitement in learning Jake was part of such a prestigious group of mountaineers quickly turned to sadness, when I read that he died in the Khumbu Icefall when a serac fell on him. He had been the rear member of three roped together to test a route in this treacherous area. The other two were rescued, but the bulk of the serac had landed on Jake. His body was not found until 1969 when it emerged from the base of the Khumbu glacier. He is buried behind the Tengboche Monastery, which looks up at Mount Everest. He was just twenty-seven years old when he died, doing what he loved most. It still saddens me—he was much too young.

SECURITY

The hospital had no security staff of its own during the time that I worked there. After the new wing was built, the facility contracted with Pinkerton to supply security, but I don't remember seeing more than one Pinkerton man covering the entire hospital on any given shift. Some of the men worked full-time, some seasonally. Many of their summer employees were teachers or students. The full-timers often seemed to be men who liked the sense of power the uniform gave them, even if they didn't carry guns.

The need for security in the 1950s and early 1960s was nothing like now. There was the occasional belligerent patient, but such people were usually controlled by the orderly and a nurse and/or doctor. During the time I worked there, I cannot recall any staff member or waiting patient being threatened with a knife or a gun, except for the guy with the arcade target and pistol. Theft happened, to be sure. Both Pat and I had our purses taken out of the admitting office one evening near Christmas—later recovered, soggy and sans cash, from the roof of the building. Even that was uncommon though predictable, given our clientele and the time of year.

The only unpleasant encounter I ever had with any of the Pinkerton men occurred early one evening when I was working an afternoon shift. We'd just admitted a psychiatric patient who was brought in by his family. It was a direct admission, meaning the patient was taken directly to the floor without stopping in emergency. The two relatives accompanying the patient were shown to my office to give me the necessary information and told to go up to the floor afterward to give the nurse and physician on duty further details about the patient. They were a little distraught, but focused enough to answer my questions.

In the middle of this process, the Pinkerton man on duty came to the door behind them. Without even a modicum of good manners, he interrupted the patient's relative in mid sentence. "Is that your car out there?" he asked brusquely. He pointed to a car right behind my office in the near-empty ER parking lot.

The man turned around and looked at him. "Yes."

"You'll have to move it. We can't have private cars in the ER lot."

I looked at this pudgy, middle-aged security-cop and said in as reasonable a tone as I could muster, "They'll move it after they've seen the doctor on the floor."

"It has to be moved NOW."

In general I tried not to lose my temper, knowing from experience that it never served me well, but this time I lost it. I stood up and leaned over the desk, my hands firmly planted on it.

"*I said*, they will move it *after* they have seen the doctor, and not until then. Now you will please leave so we can finish here and they can get to the floor."

Pudgy seemed taken aback that anyone would question—much less defy—him. After all, he was wearing a uniform! He stomped off down the hall, growling under his breath. I sat back down at the typewriter, my blood pressure still in the stratosphere, and we finished. As they went down the hall, I turned and looked out the window at the parking lot and muttered a number of expletives about stupid wannabe-cops and thanking the public safety gods that he had never made it into the police force.

Today, urban hospitals all have their own complete security staff, usually with at least one member stationed in the ER on all shifts. One of my friends who later was in charge of a newly opened ER at King County Hospital bemoaned the amount of repairs she was forced to undertake.

"We would just get it all fixed up and some idiot would come in and shoot it all up again, or there would be some huge knock-down, drag-out fight between patients and they'd break up the rooms we'd just repaired." She had been quite happily retired from there for many years when she told me that.

The days at King County Hospital in the 1950s and 1960s seem so simple in retrospect, with much less crime, fewer angry people, and almost never guns. We rarely feared for our own safety, and if we did, it was more likely to be at the hands of a psychiatric patient than someone with a weapon.

How our world has changed.

AN INVITATION TO DREAM

In the early hours of a summer morning, the sun-baked asphalt behind the ER was still radiating heat. The open window in the admitting office offered no cooling breeze. Such nights were harbingers of hot tempers, fights, and other manifestations of violence. A number of victims had already trouped through the ER before midnight but by 3 AM, with taverns and most clubs closed, our business slowed.

With chart in hand, the nurse led a tall gentleman with a newly bandaged forearm back to me and said he had offered to pay for his visit. A sutured laceration: five dollars, please. I noted he was new and had not been registered, so pulled out a stat card. A quick look at the ER chart told me he had tried to break up a fight at a nightclub and been stabbed for his efforts. His knees were almost at the level of the desktop as he folded his long legs to sit in the chair. Dark chocolate eyes sparkled when he smiled at me. His skin was as dark as his eyes, and his close-cropped hair black. His first name was Mohammed and he had a strong accent but his English was good. He was born in Anglo-Egyptian Sudan, he said, and added that he had graduated from a university in Aswan, Egypt. He gave his occupation as sailor, though he was in civilian clothes at the moment.

"I want to see the world before I take a wife and raise a family," he volunteered. "This way I can earn money while I do it."

After completing the registration and paying his bill, he did not seem in a hurry to leave. As I had taken a geography course on Africa that summer, I asked him about the area where his family lived.

"It is very beautiful," he said. "Our home is on a high plain, where my father raises many, many cattle. He is very wealthy. That is why I could go to university."

"Do you have brothers and sisters?"

"Oh, yes. I am not the eldest, so it was easier for me to go away from home, but we are a big family."

He waxed eloquent about the area of Sudan where his family lived. Clearly he loved that part of his country and had every intention of returning there to live after his wanderlust had abated. His description of his family's cattle ranch gave me visions of Montana's Big Sky country. In my mind's eye, I could imagine how glorious the night sky was, with twinkling points of light in black velvet, seeming close enough to reach out and touch.

"I've always wanted to go to Egypt," I said, perhaps a bit wistfully. I had read Emil Ludwig's *The Nile,* which had piqued my interest in its geography, as well as the wondrous archeological sites.

"Why don't you come with me on board ship?" Mohammed said, resting his elbows on the desk. "My captain reserves a few staterooms for travelers. It is not very expensive, only about $500 to go to there. Then I could take you to see Egypt, as well as the Sudan. You could meet my family, too. I know they would make you very welcome."

Such an offer! But $500 was nearly two months pay for me, and it would take at least that to return. I explained the issue to this nice man, and he suggested I might be able to borrow the money.

"The other fly in the ointment, Mohammed, is my husband. I don't think he'd be too pleased if I went off without him, especially with another man."

"Ah, of course." He smiled and sat back. "But it is a shame. I would have enjoyed showing my country to you." He stood and asked me to call a cab so he could return to his ship.

After he left, I daydreamed. The encounter brought back a flood of memories: my own trip through the Suez Canal, the *dhows* plying the canal beside the big ships, the blistering heat of the Red Sea and Aden. Oh, what an experience it would be to see the country with a native, who could translate and explain its wonders, and give me an insider's introduction to its customs. To see the pyramids, the Sphinx, the Valley of Kings—so tempting.

Then I took a deep breath and returned to reality. A cynical voice, borne from the street smarts of our clientele, questioned how innocent and genuine the offer really was, or were there possibly less savory outcomes hidden beneath. No matter. I was here, and it was time to finish my work and to call Complaints at the Police Department with tonight's group of victims, including Mohammed.

TESSA

We met B. Robert's new wife, Tessa, when they came through Seattle on their way to Vancouver, British Columbia. Federal laws did not allow her to become a resident alien until she had spent at least six months outside the country, despite her marriage to an American. She had arranged for a job at Vancouver General Hospital in Canada to wait out that period. B. Robert was still working in The Dalles, processing the results of his excavations at Celilo Falls for the University of Washington.

Tessa was a big-boned, buxom woman with a ready laugh and a smile that lit up the blue eyes behind her glasses. Bare-legged and wearing Birkenstocks, her wardrobe bespoke comfort, not high fashion. As we got better acquainted, I was most taken by her calm, totally unpretentious manner. Her English was lightly accented, and her choice of words was sometimes a mixture of her native Dutch or the French or Flemish she spoke fluently. This occasionally made conversations quite interesting.

"When B. Bob and I were first living together in The Dalles," she told us once, "we went to a drug store for something to drink. It was so hot and dry outside and he had to go back into the field that afternoon. I asked him to drive me home so I could take a douche. He kind of laughed and looked a little red in the face. The man behind the counter was grinning at him. I didn't know what was so funny.

"'Do you know what "douche" means?' he said to me when we got into the car. I told him of course I did. When he explained what it means to Americans, I just laughed and told him it means "shower" in French. He told me 'Use "shower" from now on,' so other people wouldn't mistake my meaning." She chuckled. "*Hawt*! It took me awhile to realize how easily embarrassed Americans are."

By March of 1957, when The Dalles dam was completed, Tessa's exile was finished and she returned to B. Robert with a legal resident visa. Later that summer, they gathered up the fruits of his labors and returned to Seattle, he to complete his Master's degree and she to find work. Bob, Jan, and I had moved to a new, smaller apartment over a tavern, and the couple stayed with us briefly until they found a place.

One evening while they were staying with us, Jan invited a man over to play cards. Chet was about thirty-five years old, dressed in slacks, white shirt, and tie even on that hot summer evening, making him seem a bit priggish. The two Roberts were shirtless and in shorts and Jan and I were wearing shorts and tank tops. Tessa had donned baby-doll pajamas. All of our outfits were more befitting the ninety degrees in the apartment. The men and Jan were playing poker at the dining table.

Tessa leaned her voluptuous, scantily clad self over her husband's shoulder to see what cards he held. Chet, sitting next to him, glanced over and turned beet red. My Bob, who had dealt the hand, asked him if he wanted any cards, but poor Chet was speechless. He fumbled, almost losing his cards, and broke out in a sweat. Finally he shook his head. The other two men could barely stop themselves from bursting out laughing. Jan smiled as surreptitiously as she could manage, but I had to leave the room altogether. Tessa was totally oblivious.

Fortuitously, a position for a medical record clerk at King County Hospital came open about that time. Tessa applied and got the job.

After her initial training on days, she requested the evening shift. Hardworking, friendly, and even-tempered, she fit in handily. Dinners at work were a time for gabbing, and her stories were always interesting. She spoke openly about the war years in Holland.

"My father was an artist and too old for the Nazis to draft him," she told us one night. "We hid a Jewish brother and sister, and had to move around a lot. The living was hard, because there wasn't much to eat for anyone. We spent part of the war on an island off the north coast of Holland. That was better in some ways. The people on the island grew their own food, and it was so small the Nazis didn't care much about it. The Jewish children were safer there."

The staff in Medical Records warmed to her uniformly. The only time anyone said anything remotely negative was during a hot spell when everyone was perspiring. Tessa wore no deodorant and the girls working around her brought it to their supervisor's attention. Tessa was surprised.

"We never wore it at home. These are natural smells of people; why would you disguise it?"

Someone donated a stick of deodorant and she used it, but thought it was silly to make such a fuss.

During the holidays, sweet goodies made their appearance in all the departments, including Medical Records. Although Tessa had no interest in ordinary cooking, she loved making truffles. Everyone agreed that her truffles were better than you could buy in the stores. Melt-in-the-mouth chocolate rolled in sweetened cocoa powder--they disappeared as soon as the box was opened.

Then a new young German woman named Isabel started on evenings. She was the wife of a German physician, who was taking classes at the medical school to prepare for the examinations that would allow him to get his American license to practice. When Tessa and Isabel were introduced, the tension between them was palpable. Suddenly World War II seemed not quite over. They were polite to each other on the job, but Tessa had little interaction with her aside from that.

The rest of us understood the Dutch and Germans had been enemies quite recently, but the war had ended and we hoped it would not erupt in our neutral American territory here. Isabel told us living in Nazi Germany had not been any more a picnic than any other country in Europe during the war. I asked her once if her husband had been a Nazi. She looked at me rather sadly.

"Yes, he was. He had no choice. If we wanted to survive, he had to join them. But he was a doctor, so he didn't have to fight. That didn't mean we had any special treatment. In fact, toward the end of the war, when the bombing was every day, every night, there was hardly any food in Berlin anywhere. We had to eat grass—there wasn't anything else toward the end. It left me with kidney problems."

Away from work, I asked Tessa why she felt so negatively about Isabel.

"I don't want to have anything to do with her." Her tone of voice was cold, so unlike the woman I knew. "*Hawt*! Her husband was a Nazi. She was one, too. I can't forgive what the Nazis did."

"But, Tessa, you've heard what she's said about her own experiences. What choice did they have?"

"I know what she says. I don't believe it. The doctors got better treatment than the rest, just like the high military officers. He was a doctor for the Nazis. I know some of the things they did. I'll work with her but I cannot be friends."

For many months the tension between them remained before gradually Tessa thawed. Although a real friendship never developed, the hostility subsided. Isabel quit as soon as her husband went into private practice.

Tessa's first child was born during the time she worked at King County Hospital. During those first weeks after the baby was born before she came back to work, money was very scarce. There was one month when they had no heat in their little apartment. B. Robert was on a dig out of state with barely enough money to support himself on the site, and hospital benefits did not extend to pay while on maternity leave. Dutch stoicism and her experiences in the war years paid off. Tessa stretched their meager budget to pay for food and rent, but not the expensive oil for their central heater. I gave her a bassinet and some blankets and clothes for the baby, and marveled at her adaptability. The cold did not seem to bother her; she just added sweaters. Breast-feeding took care of the baby's food needs. At last B. Robert came back from his dig, and Tessa could return to work. Ordinary life began again.

Tessa continued to work at the hospital until B. Robert completed his Master's and got a job teaching at the University of Idaho in Pocatello. Her life during the war and innate frugality stood her in good stead with her husband's chosen profession of archeology. Always on a slim budget, and often on digs in camping mode for an entire summer with their children, she found their lifestyle forever interesting.

We remained life-long friends.

A WALK ON THE DARK SIDE

One frigid January night, a farmer brought his wife in. They came in an old truck, he in clothes obviously yanked on in haste, his pale-blue eyes with the foggy look of interrupted sleep. She still wore her nightgown and slippers, a worn brown coat thrown over her shoulders.

A neighbor had found her wandering down the country road in her nightgown, no shoes or even a bathrobe to keep out the bone-chilling mist. Her husband, soundly asleep, had not been aware that she'd gotten out of bed, much less left the house. He was very troubled when the neighbor finally was able to wake him and explain what had happened. It was the third time in a month that she had been brought back from such a midnight walk. Even though he had to get up before dawn for chores, he sensed she could not wait until morning to be seen by a doctor.

As I entered the room to register the patient with my clipboard in hand, the husband stood up. It was a courtesy seldom seen in our ER. He held a battered hat in his hands, and nervously turned it round and round. His rumpled overalls smelled of barn. He was a big man, probably in his early fifties, with receding brown hair beginning to turn gray.

His wife sat quietly in the examining room chair, seemingly unaware of her surroundings. She was big-boned and thin. Her shoulders were broad and her arms muscular. High cheekbones gave her a vaguely Asian appearance, belied by her long, straight blond hair, which fell below her shoulders, still damp from her nighttime stroll. With her large, brilliant blue eyes and her tall, big-boned frame, the word that sprang instantly to mind was "Valkyrie." I glanced quickly at the name on the ER sheet and asked her the necessary questions. She spoke with a distinct accent, but her English was good. Although she understood what was being said, she seemed unable to focus and the answers came slowly. When I got her to birth date, I had to prompt her for the year. She just looked at me blankly. I turned to her husband.

"She's 41," he responded.

"Are you a citizen, Mrs. Cole?" When she nodded her head, I added, "How long have you been in the United States?"

As if she were counting the years one by one, she finally answered. "Fifteen years." When I had finished, I gave her the form to look over, to make sure it was right, and then sign at the bottom. She looked at it for a long time and finally slowly signed her name. She put down the pen and folded her hands on the clipboard, staring off into space. I gently extracted the board. She did not move her hands at all.

An hour later, the doctor and the couple came down to my office. Mr. Cole was talking to the doctor, and appeared worried.

"I don't know," he said. "It doesn't sound like my wife belongs in a place like that. What would they do to her up there?"

The doctor reassured him that she would be well cared for, and stressed how important it was that his wife get help without delay. "She needs a psychiatrist now," he concluded. "It will only get worse if she doesn't get help immediately."

Perhaps it was the word *psychiatrist* that did it; perhaps he couldn't admit that there was anything mentally wrong with his wife.

Whatever thoughts went into his decision, the farmer straightened up and said firmly, "My wife is going home with me. I can't put her in any nut ward."

He took his wife's arm and led her, tall and wraith-like in her white nightgown, back down the hallway to the exit. The doctor walked with them, trying to persuade the husband to admit her into the hospital but to no avail. She did not appear to hear any of their conversation.

As the department quieted down, I went out to chat with the nurses.

"It's a real shame about that Finnish woman," one of them commented. "Her husband obviously was upset by the idea that *his* wife could be a candidate for the funny farm, but I'll bet she's admitted somewhere by the end of the month. She's definitely decompensating."

It didn't take even that long. The very next night the farmer brought his wife back. This time she was not responding at all. If someone sat her in a chair, she did not move from it. When the nurse held her arm to take her pulse and blood pressure, she left the arm in the same position after the nurse was through. She no longer answered any questions, or, indeed, said anything at all. Her gaze was fixed straight ahead, her wide blue eyes staring unseeing.

It took the same doctor who had seen her the night before just five minutes to send them back to me to do the admission book work. This time the husband was meek and did not argue.

"Please do something to help her," he said. "I want my wife back--I didn't know it would get this bad. I don't understand what's happening to her."

The diagnosis read "catatonic schizophrenia, acute."

"I know it's hard to accept," the doctor told Mr. Cole. "But you did the right thing by bringing her in. She is at least on the road to getting the help she needs."

Although we non-physicians were not privy to the follow-up on patients, I did learn later that she had been discharged to a psychiatric hospital.

What caused this woman's break with reality? What kind of relationship did she have with her husband? Did she ever come out of her catatonic state enough to respond and tell her side? That was the only unsatisfactory part of my job: I never got to read the end of the story.

OOPS!

We all make mistakes. Some are critical, some embarrassing, some barely noteworthy. They happen as often in hospitals as anywhere else.

Called to register a new patient for a stat admission, I grabbed the clipboard and went to the nurses' station. In the entry hallway Helen handed me a stat card with the diagnosis of kidney failure already signed by the intern, and pointed to an elderly female patient on a gurney. A man I judged to be around fifty stood beside her. The patient was pale, though not the blue-gray of cyanosis: her skin appeared to be covered with a grayish powder. There seemed to be almost no substance beneath the blankets carefully wrapped around her. Her eyes were closed, and it was clear I would get no answers from her. She appeared to be seventy or eighty years old. I turned to the man accompanying her. Not wanting to ask information already available, I ignored the name, address and birthdate and went on to the other data I needed.

"Are you a relative?" I asked, noting with a quick glance at the ER chart as he replied that his last name and hers were the same. When he nodded, I continued pen poised over the square for relationship, "Your mother?"

He heaved a resigned sigh. "No, she's my wife."

Embarrassed, I apologized, and checked the birthdate—she was, indeed, only about fifty herself.

Later that evening I asked Helen why she appeared so much older than her true age.

"She had uremic frost," she said. "That's when the kidney function is so bad that waste products collect even in the sweat glands. What made her skin look gray were whitish urea crystals that form as a result. You don't see it very often."

Another pathophysiologic tidbit learned—and another lesson about making assumptions.

Oops.

Jenny was one of the evening medical transcriptionists. Her desk was in front of the windows of our new Medical Record department. Black-haired and bubbly, she was known to keep up a muttered one-sided conversation with the doctor she was transcribing, particularly if the recording was difficult. This night she was talking to herself as usual, when she took off the earphones and bent down to untie her shoes.

"Boy, it's hot tonight," she said to no one in particular. "They must have turned up the heat—the floor is so warm."

The others in the department just looked at her. The clerks on duty were not stationary long enough to notice. But a little while later, Jenny remarked on the warm floor again.

"It's getting hotter. Doesn't anyone else feel it?"

The evening supervisor, a few desks away, bent down to feel the floor. "It's not unusually warm here," she commented. She got up and went over to Jenny's desk, and put her hand on the floor. "You're right. It shouldn't be that warm. I wonder what's happening."

The supervisor picked up the phone and called Engineering. The responding engineer went down to the file room in the basement, and then out into the basement hallway. Smoke was seeping under the door of the room next to the basement file room--linen storage--which was directly under Jenny's desk. He immediately called the Fire Department.

However, when they arrived the engineer had disappeared and when they tried the doors on that end of the building, they all were locked. In the ER, we were unaware of any problems until a fireman came through the door, the only open entrance at that hour.

Finally, this Chinese fire drill got straightened out and the fire doused. The cause was discovered to be a cigarette left smoldering on a shelf full of cotton sheets, its owner apparently having gone home. There was no rule against smoking in the hospital in those days, but I suspect the person who smoked there did not have a job the next day.

Oops.

CHANGES

Nineteen fifty-seven brought a number of changes. By the end of winter quarter, I had finished all the requirements for my bachelor's degree. Bob had quit his carpentry job and tried a quarter at the university, but had been unimpressed with his classes and didn't go back. After some searching, he found a job as evening dispatcher for Yellow Cab.

Jan married and moved out of our apartment, but did not quit her job at the hospital.

Nancy was firmly ensconced as evening charge nurse in the ER.

I learned early on that Bob had a few passionate hates: policemen, lawyers, and politicians. One night Bob and I were on our way home from work when a cop pulled us over. I recognized the officer and quickly got out of the car, still in my work uniform. I wanted to forestall any sarcastic comments that might create a preventable issue.

"Hi, Roger, what's the problem?"

He looked at me for a moment, ticket pad in hand, and then nodded as he recognized me. "Your back tail light is out. You'll want to get that fixed. I'll just give you a warning this time, but next time it will be a ticket if it hasn't been replaced." No smiles, all business. Roger was an honest, letter-of-the-law cop, and from all I'd seen of him, without much of a sense of humor. Bob put in a new light the next day.

But there was one officer I'd met through work that Bob made an exception for, perhaps because he was black and smarter than most of the other cops with whom Bob had had contact. Matt was a detective of whom we saw a fair amount in the ER. Another officer, David, was a regular on Complaints. He had been taken off the street because of disability, and sometimes chafed at his assignment. Both these men tended to be more easy-going than some of the others, and the two were good friends.

I don't recall how the event came about, but one night Matt and David came to our apartment to play cards after work. Bob was working for Yellow Cab then, all of us on swing shift. About midnight, we congregated at our place.

"We're going to play by *my* rules," Matt announced, taking off his gun belt and dropping it beside him on the floor as Bob went to get the cards. He turned and took a quick look, but Matt's grin reassured him. I don't remember much about the rest of the night except there was a lot of laughter until the wee hours.

Then in midsummer, after an embarrassing fainting spell in a restaurant, I discovered I was pregnant. Bob was delighted, which relieved me, remembering Nazir's ambivalence. Nevertheless, I had serious trepidations about my abilities as a mother. Bob kept reassuring me that I would do fine, and he was right there to help. Perhaps it was that which made this pregnancy a benign one with no morning sickness, It was smooth sailing all the way through.

We gave a big New Year's Eve party at our little apartment over the Reservoir Tavern to celebrate the last of our "couple-dom" before parenthood overtook us. Bob had prepared by buying a bottle of something alcoholic with each paycheck—there was no way we could run out of booze. We had about twelve people in that small place, plus our neighbors in the next apartment and some from the university. Our rowdy party went on as long as the noisy celebrations in the tavern below, and a good time was had by all.

In February of 1958, our daughter, Lisa, was born, and we barely made it to the hospital in time. She was definitely her father's girl, with his dark hair and brown eyes, and the same plump, dimpled cheeks when she smiled. Like Nish, she cried a lot, but Bob took an active part in her care and his willing participation made it much easier for me to maintain my perspective. He recruited his mother, who lived a couple of miles south of the hospital, to take care of her when I returned to work.

I went back to the job full-time on swing shift, alternating between Admitting and Medical Records. Pat by then was also pregnant, and after she had her baby, I took over the Admitting Office on evenings for the rest of my tenure at KCH.

Not long after my return to work, Bob took and passed the civil service test for Seattle City Light, tenth out of a group of over one hundred applicants. He was now on day shift, which lessened the time Lisa had to be with her grandparents.

The remaining three years of my time at King County Hospital are something of a blur—with raising our daughter and working full-time. A few mini-events still pop out.

First was the evening when one of the nurses left the keys on the drug room counter and shut the door, which automatically locked. Nancy called Dick, still skinny as a toothpick, who managed to squeeze himself between the close-placed bars of the drug room window and retrieve the keys. How he did that without breaking ribs, I'll never know.

The second was the night the wife of one South American country's consul was brought in, having been beaten by her husband. She arrived with two bags of clothes and a lot of jewelry. When she was admitted to the observation ward in ER, the orderly had to catalog her belongings. He came back shaking his head.

"She must have thousands of dollars worth of emeralds in her suitcase," he said, "and I had to list them all as green stones." She was released sometime the next day, but not back to her husband.

The third was a handsome black couple, dressed in their Sunday best, whose four-year-old boy had been running and fell, hitting his forehead on a pew in the church. A small laceration had been cleaned and sutured, and they insisted on paying their bill. The young man stood quietly with his parents, nattily dressed in a light blue suit, vest, white shirt and black bow tie. The sight was such a shocking contrast to our usual clientele, it still stands out clearly in my memory.

The University of Washington Hospital opened in 1959, and not long after that Jan quit King County Hospital and got a job in the Medical Transcription Department there. I talked to her after she had been working there for a time, and she encouraged me to apply. "The money is better," she said, "and it's really interesting work."

So in 1961, I applied and got a job in that department, to begin in June on the day shift as a trainee.

On my last day at King County Hospital, my husband sent me an orchid. He was really happy to have me working the same shift as his at last.

I had chosen the path and looked forward to the next adventure.

WHAT BECAME OF US

Those of us working toward degrees at the university finally achieved our goals. The three in the graduate school of social work—Sam, another orderly, and the orderly's LPN wife—went on to jobs in their chosen field.

Sam returned to King County Hospital as a social worker, and held positions in other government agencies as well. He married a young woman with his father's blessing, and became a pillar of his community, receiving many awards for his volunteer activities in his church and former high school.

B. Robert finished his Masters in Archeology while **Tessa** continued to work at the hospital. They left when he joined the faculty at the University of Idaho at Pocatello. He ultimately became the curator of the museum there. Tessa worked off and on, and became a local volunteer for UNICEF.

B. Robert maintained a consulting service for the State of Idaho when artifacts or human bones were discovered on building construction or road project sites. His job was to determine whether these were Native American sites that would need further archeological investigation. In the 1990s, B. Robert got another MA in clinical psychology, and then his PhD. I teased this prickly pear of a man unmercifully about his choice of major, but celebrated his accomplishments nevertheless.

Through the years, we visited almost yearly; either they came to Seattle or Bob and I went to Pocatello. Tessa's birthday and mine were one day apart, and one of us usually called the other. I did not hear from her in October of 2008, and thought perhaps she hadn't called because I had been to see them earlier in the year. However, another year went by without any word from either of them. Early in 2010, after a Christmas card had gone unanswered, I received a call from their son, who told me Tessa had developed meningitis three months after I had last seen them, which left her blind, deaf, and paralyzed. In a state where assisted death was illegal, she had pleaded with B. Robert to put her out of her misery, and he had obliged, five days after her birthday. Then he took his own life. The news media termed it a "mercy killing." Indeed, for this active woman even the short period before she died must have been a living hell. It broke my heart—for both of them.

Dan. Years later, I ran into Dan when he was a practicing attorney. By then I was in charge of the legal desk at Virginia Mason Hospital and occasionally went on depositions for cases concerning our patients. When Dan was the attorney involved, he made a point of taking the deposition at the hospital instead of my going to his office, which was the normal routine. After I started teaching, our friendship continued. When our schedules aligned, I snagged him as a guest lecturer for my legal class. He was one of the few people outside of Medical Records with whom I maintained a working relationship from that time so long ago.

Helen. She left the hospital a little before I did, and we lost touch. Working on this book I thought about her often, and so one night, on a whim, I searched for her name on the internet. To my surprise, it came up with an address and phone number She was still in the area, so I called and we met for lunch. I told her about my project and that

I'd like to do a chapter on her. She wasn't sure, but she agreed to think about it. Two weeks later, we met in her comfortable home way out in the country at the end of a dirt road.

She filled me in on events she remembered, and told me about her jobs after she left ER. For a while she worked as a special nurse caring for individual patients at home or in other hospitals around Seattle. There was one patient she remembered well: the first woman to graduate from University of Washington's law school. "Tough lady," she commented.

She then worked at Ballard Hospital, initially in the nursery, and later in their intensive care unit, one of the first to open in Seattle. One day, the pharmacist asked her to start IV's. She was so good at it, he asked her to do that full-time. It was something they didn't have as a specialty in those days. That was her job until she retired at seventy-two.

"What did you like best about nursing?" I asked her.

"I think it was the variety," she said after a moment of thought. "There was always something new to learn, and you met so many interesting people."

I reached the end of my questions, and closed my notebook. We chatted about news of mutual acquaintances. I looked at the clock, and realized how fast the afternoon has sped by. We smiled wrinkly smiles at each other, and I promised to send her my first draft as soon as I got it done.

My time with her after making contact so many years later was brief. We had arranged to meet for lunch, but she called to say she was ill and would call me when she felt better. When a month had gone by without word, I called the number she had given me and discovered she had died a few days after her ninetieth birthday. I was so glad to have had the short time with her.

Nancy, however, is an on-going saga. Very much alive and well, a master gardener, she still plans social events and is active with the doctors and nurses with whom she worked. Nancy and I have traveled together a couple of times since her retirement, and her itchy foot has covered a good share of the world. Our friendship continues.

It took me a bit longer to figure out what I wanted to be when I grew up, but King County Hospital turned out to be the bottom rung on the ladder of my career. The next rung was the jump into medical transcription at the University of Washington Medical Center, where I joined my previous roommate and coworker, Jan.

In 1963, our son, Garth, was born, and I went back on evenings at the University, working from 6 PM to 2 AM. Bob was not overly happy with that arrangement, but at least one of us was always home with the children.

A chance remark by my supervisor, six years after that, led me to the program for certification as a Medical Record Librarian. (That title morphed into Registered Record Administrator and then Registered Healthcare Information Administrator—it took a long time before the profession figured out what it really did.) For six years as assistant supervisor of medical records, I had charge of the hospital section of Medical Records Department at Virginia Mason Medical Center.

The summer of 1970 was momentous for me: Nish came back into my life. Nazir was in town with Nish and his English wife, Pat, teaching a summer program on Indian music in the Music department at the University of Washington, a career in which he had blossomed. He dropped Nish off one afternoon at our house, promising to pick her up after his class. I was excited but terrified, deeply afraid how she would react to me. Nish was unsure what to expect—would she be welcome or not? There had never been any explanation why I let her go. After so many years, seeing this young girl, now seventeen, tall with long black hair, her father's deep brown, long-lashed eyes, looking so much like him, I was almost breathless. I wanted to hug her but was afraid of being rebuffed, so limited my welcome to a big smile. I have no idea what either of us said, but somehow we both got through those first awkward moments and settled in to get reacquainted. Garth was entranced, but Lisa found this big sister intimidating— she was beautiful and her English accent made her seem so sophisticated and worldly. Nish was less confident than she seemed, she told me later. By the time her father returned, we had determined she would call me Lynn, and she was Nish to all of us.

I wanted to meet her the following day, but we were scheduled to leave on vacation, and Bob would not put it off a single day, angry that I would even suggest it. Nazir and family were still here when we returned, however, and we were able to connect again before they went back to the University of Windsor in Canada. The contact had been made and proved to be the beginning of many visits to solidify our newfound relationship.

In 1975, I moved on to Shoreline Community College, finishing out my career as program director for medical record technicians, medical transcriptionists, and medical secretaries at Shoreline Community College.

By 1980, however, Bob and I were divorced, but this time there was no question in my mind—the children would stay with me. Even program directors at community colleges don't make a great deal of money: with Bob's exit went more than half the family income. This meant finding a second job, and I fell back on my old skills as a medical transcriptionist on the weekends. Fortuitous in some ways—it gave me more credibility as an instructor, as well as keeping the family solvent.

After I retired from my teaching job, I kept the part-time job I had had as medical transcriptionist during the last fifteen years at Shoreline, finally retiring completely at eighty-two.

Being part of the healthcare community was hard to give up, even then.

FROM FLINTSTONES TO JETSONS

Some years ago, my then six-year-old grandson asked me, "Did you have radio when you were young, Grandma?" We were at that moment watching Star Trek on television.

"Yes, but we didn't have TV," I answered. His question reminded me how far inventions had come, and with almost logarithmic speed.

King County Hospital in the 1940s and 1950s was close to the pre-television era. The contrast between then and now is stark. Dr. Audrey Young, in her 2009 book about the medical center, *House of Hope and Fear*, details many of the changes in the physical plant as well as operational differences. The current emergency department, located in yet another addition (the East Hospital), is greatly expanded, with a larger observation ward that substitutes as a holding area for patients waiting for admission. There is a radio room for contact with incoming Medic One ambulances, another with an ever-changing board for determining bed availability status in other hospitals around Seattle, and many more examining rooms. I would guess that all three shifts of doctors and nurses from my day in the 1950s would probably barely staff one shift of the Emergency Department today.

The old electric typewriters have been replaced with computers and laptops. Paper records have been replaced by computerized electronic records (to the discomfiture of a few older physicians less comfortable with computers). Overhead paging systems have given way to pocket pagers and cell phones.

The original two buildings have had multiple accretions, emptying the original hospital of patients, in large part because of earthquake building codes that were too expensive to implement.

Now called Harborview Medical Center, the campus consists of:

* The original hospital, now designated the Center Tower, on 9th Avenue
* East Clinic (the first addition, completed in 1955)
* West Clinic fronting on 8th Avenue
* West Hospital, fronting on 8th Avenue
* East Hospital on 9th and Jefferson, with the Emergency Department on the ground level
* Norm Maleng Building, on 9th & Jefferson, across the street from the East Hospital
* The Ninth and Jefferson Building, opposite the Norm Maleng Building
* The Research and Training Building, across from the East Clinic
* The Patricia Steel Building, on Broadway at Jefferson.
* The Heliport located west of the West Clinic.
* View Park west of the West Hospital, with its serene vista over Puget Sound to the Olympic Mountains.
* The original nurses' building across from the Center Tower remains, but is in limbo. Some want to tear it down and create an open green space in its place. Others would like to keep it for its unique architecture and historical importance.

Outside of the physical changes, events in the social and political arenas, as well as medical advances, have altered Harborview's economic landscape.

In 1965 and 1966, Medicare and Medicaid came into being. For the first time Harborview could get at least some payment for many of the patients who had been one hundred percent charity care. Reimbursement rates, especially for Medicaid, are notoriously low, but offset by the acceptance of patients with "regular" insurance. There was a brief exodus from the hospital after Medicaid allowed patients to be seen in other hospitals, but Harborview's regulars soon returned, having found themselves less welcome in the private settings. And despite the increase in reimbursement, there were still too many patients who fell in the cracks between Medicaid/Medicare and private insurance.

In 1967, the University of Washington Medical School took over management of Harborview in an arrangement made with King County (which still owns the property and physical plant).

In 1970, Medic One came into operation. It was spurred on by the work of Dr. Frank Pantridge, an Irish cardiologist who developed a portable ventricular defibrillator for use in ambulances, and Dr. Leonard Cobb, a University of Washington cardiologist, who, in conjunction with Gordon Vickery, then head of the Seattle Fire Department, developed the concept of home-to-hospital cardiac resuscitation. It was housed at Harborview, putting Seattle on the national map. Because they already had some emergency medical training, fire fighters were a logical starting group for more in depth medical training.

About the same time, Dr. Michael Copass arrived on the scene, bringing the hospital up to a Level One trauma center--the only one in a five-state area (Washington, Alaska, Montana, Idaho and

Wyoming). Even in my antediluvian time, ambulance drivers and police brought accidents and serious injuries to Harborview unless the patient specifically requested a different hospital. Now, with a heliport in place, patients can be brought in by air from all over the Northwest, including Alaska.

The Harborview Burn Center is one of the largest in the United States, and has pioneered inventive treatments that have greatly improved burn victims' survivability. (I suspect the use of even "sterile" maggots for burn debridement is not yet the norm, however.)

Some of the programs developed at Harborview are unique to the area. In 1973, the Center for Sexual Assault was established and remains one of the programs most experienced in the country for medical care and counseling these victims and their families. The hospital was also an early provider for treatment of HIV/AIDS patients. University of Washington Center for AIDS research is based at Harborview, one of the few AIDS research programs in the country.

A kerfuffle arose in 2014 between the University of Washington Medical School and King County when a decision was made to close the primary care clinics at HMC. King County still owns Harborview and under state law is operated by a board of trustees appointed by the King County executive and its Council. The board of trustees weighed in and demanded a review of the University of Washington management contract. The board felt the key mission of serving the poor had been jeopardized.[6] However, as of this writing, a new ten-year contract between King County and the University of Washington has been signed, assuring that the poor and indigent will still be cared for without regard to their ability to pay. Harborview's clinics will not be closed.[7] With its expansion, it serves far more people in many new ways, but its core philosophy is unique in the city and will be maintained.

Of all the hospitals in Seattle where I have worked or been privy to their operations (which is most of them), my heart remains with Harborview.

SOME THOUGHTS ABOUT THE FUTURE

For the public at large, the results of changes in health care have improved survival significantly through technology and greater coverage by insurance. Nonetheless, despite the United States having the most expensive medical care on the planet, the outcomes are a mixed bag. Amnesty International's evaluation of pregnancy-related complications and death places the United States behind forty other countries, with death during childbirth five times greater than that in Greece.[8] (Getting religion and politics out of obstetrics and gynecology might help!) Studies of outcome differences between Canada and the United States are also variable: breast and cervical cancer outcomes are better in the US,[9] while Canada does better with colorectal cancers and leukemia[10] despite the care being considerably less expensive.

With the passage of the Affordable Care Act in 2010, the losses Harborview suffered fell: the expansion of Medicaid covered many of those low-income people who could not afford regular insurance. By 2014, the losses had dropped from nearly $220 million to a projected seven million[11]—significant, but not zero. Other provisions of the ACA, however, may penalize Harborview's bottom line for higher infection rates and higher rate of return for the same condition within too short a time after the patient's discharge. Such provisions do not take into consideration the unique nature of their patient mix: the homeless (who may still not have any insurance) and the poverty-level employed, who, even with subsidized insurance, don't make enough to take care of their health. These are the people who end up at Harborview when things go sour for them. Too, many physicians in the community will not accept Medicaid and some will not even accept new Medicare patients because of the low reimbursement rates.

There is speculation that there will be too few primary care physicians to serve a growing insured public, to say nothing of too few nurses and other primary caregivers like nurse practitioners and physicians' assistants. How can the pipeline for new practitioners in these fields be increased, and how can we encourage them to stay in the profession(s)? New ways to fund medical school must be found. If a graduate is in debt for several hundred thousand dollars, s/he is unlikely to opt for primary care where the greatest need is, choosing instead the more lucrative specialties. But Dr. Sandeep Jauhar, a cardiologist with a hospital on Long Island, New York, points out "Specialists are paid more than primary care physicians, but they are also less autonomous because, unlike primary care physicians, they are dependent on other physicians for referrals. So there is tremendous pressure on specialists to keep referral sources happy."[12] This means survival for the specialists but not always value-added for the patient.

The fee-for-service stance taken by insurance companies and Medicare/Medicaid is a catch-22: the more patients they can see in a day, the better the reimbursement, which again does not necessarily contribute to quality patient care or satisfaction for either doctor or patient.

Physicians are paid for reading (think "analyzing") x-rays, EKGs, echocardiograms, and all manner of lab tests. The patient may then be recalled for an office appointment to explain those results. Although the cost of medical malpractice insurance is coming down,[13] the fear of a lawsuit often leads to ordering tests that might not be necessary—the cover-your-posterior response. Additionally, some Medicare mandated protocols require certain tests to be performed, in the interest of maintaining quality control, although medical judgment in individual cases might deem otherwise. This leads to higher costs, as well as greater reimbursement; it also takes some of the doctor's autonomy away.

Another cause for acute dissatisfaction among physicians and nurses is the monumental increase in paperwork simply to get paid by insurance companies and Medicare/Medicaid. That alone has driven many physicians to leave the field altogether, especially the older ones. It has also left the newer doctors more disillusioned about their chosen profession. Some doctors now encourage their children to think of other kinds of jobs, and not to consider medicine at all.

The high cost of medical school, falling reimbursement rates from government and private insurers, and the amount of required paperwork have all conspired to cast a pall on prospective students' interest in the profession. Reimbursement formulas are needed to better reward family practice/pediatrics and internal medicine at baseline. Further, the need to adhere to mandated protocols ("cookbook medicine") when the doctor may feel it inappropriate is yet another perceived disadvantage. These issues will need to be addressed in order to maintain a physician pool large enough to manage the increased number of patients.

"Medicare for all" was a rallying cry by many during the fight for the Affordable Care Act. If this were to be achieved, there could be significant savings for the healthcare costs--but only if it also came with revisions to Medicare policies, not the least of which would be negotiated drug prices. The ability and willingness to take on the entrenched drug and healthcare insurance industries which dictate prices to consumers is such a political hot potato, it is not likely to happen any time soon. Realistically, it cannot be a free system to all comers, but the current "whatever the traffic will bear" stance will bankrupt either consumers or the government—or both. The ACA has taken a few baby steps ahead, but there is still a long way to go. Even with a minimalist view, however, such a system is predicated on the consumer's ability to make a living wage. Incomes need to be adequate for patients to be able to maintain their health through adequate nutrition, housing, and access to health care. For that to happen, the ideal would be a single payer system, in which all basic care was available to everyone for a rational percentage of their income. For the wealthier, who can afford greater perks, the concierge style care is available even now [14].

The single payer system presupposes salaries of physicians would be negotiated with the government. The likelihood of the medical profession being willing to do that is probably low, although it has been done locally with groups like the Mayo Clinic and Cleveland Clinic.[15] This removes the financial impetus to overtest.

Patients, too, need to adjust their expectations to a more realistic view of what can be achieved through medical care. Not everything can be cured by a pill, despite the drug companies' enticing advertisements. Nor are all bad outcomes are the result of medical malpractice—some really are the result of unexpected anatomic or physiologic variances that could not be anticipated or did not respond to carefully tailored treatment. And sometimes the patient's own actions (or inaction) may have contributed.

Of course, this doesn't begin to touch on the political scene that puts roadblocks in the way of a single payer plan, which opponents call, pejoratively, "socialized medicine," Many in the medical profession balk at any idea of health care that resembles that in England and Canada (and indeed, much of Europe), but the discussion is changing. Dr. Young notes that some form of "universal systems of coverage has begun at the state level in Oregon, Hawaii, Maine and Massachusetts."[16] And as of 2016, the push is beginning in Washington state for single payer coverage. The pushback from insurance and pharmaceutical companies will be formidable undoubtedly. My guess is that places like Harborview would welcome it.

The electronic health record (EHR) was pushed prior to the ACA, and now is mandated. Not only is it a politically neutral step toward universal healthcare, but over time, a cost-cutting one. I know of no hospital without some kind of electronic information system. Administrative and billing data has long been computerized. Upgrading to a total healthcare data system to include the patient record is expensive, and smaller rural hospitals have a harder time affording this, but likely will eventually get there. Down-time time for back-up, equipment failure, data loss through mistakes (how often have you hit delete by accident?), and even data theft by hackers throw wrenches into the works, but I don't see that stopping progress in this area. Savings have come from the elimination of the paper records and the file rooms in which they were stored, as well as the need for file clerks to process it. Lab test results are entered once and will not have to be repeated because a paper report was lost. Data entered can be read by anyone with the need to know, wherever they may be, without waiting for a paper record to be found and sent from one place to another. Even the patient can access his own data in most places where such systems exist. Timely transfer between treating physicians makes for better patient care. Confidentiality is readily monitored, keeping out those who do not need to utilize the information, and tracking those who try to access it without authorization.

I would be flogged at sunrise in a public square if I did not note the changes to my own profession that have occurred in this same time period. Medical record practitioners went from being managers of paper records and confidentiality to managers of major health data systems and consultants to private and government agencies relating to patient information privacy (Health Information Portability and Accountability Act--HIPAA) and to Medicare/Medicaid and the Office of the Inspector General for issues related to health-data quality and integrity. Those professionals who did the coding of diagnoses and operations, once reserved for research, became the linchpin for billing, elevating theirs from just another clerical job to a key position in the financial well-being of their institution.

The health information manager is increasingly the interface between the patient, physician, and institution, and all those entities who want the documentation to pay bills, do research, develop systems, and minimize risk to all the above. The demand for this job will likely increase, but we need to be sure that the vision does not remain narrow, but embraces the larger perspective of healthcare generally.

Perhaps when private insurance, pharmaceutical, and healthcare companies can get away from being beholden to stockholders first and their customers second, the cost of health care can be brought down. The conflict of interest between stockholders and healthcare companies, and the clientele they serve as well as the workers they employ is an increasing problem. For example, in order to maintain investor interest and a positive bottom line, Community Health Systems, which owns over two hundred hospitals in twenty-nine states, has instituted cost-cutting measures that result in understaffing, thereby endangering patient care.[17] Personnel costs are among the most expensive facets of running a hospital, and the first to be chipped away.

It is also in the political arena where we must confront the issues of having clean air to breathe, clean water to drink, and food that is not contaminated with pesticides and drugs given to the food animals--all of which impacts the health of our nation.

We all need to be activists in ensuring everyone--at every economic level--is able to live the healthiest life possible. This progress will likely start at the local level first—at places like Harborview and other public hospitals like it—where the first priority has always been to serve the person with the most need.

ACKNOWLEDGMENTS

This book has been so long in the writing, I'm sure I will leave out many who gave me advice and helped by critiquing its bits and pieces—a multitude in the twenty years it has taken to finally finish. Initial thanks go to Ariele Huff who encouraged me to write down my memories of the experiences I had of Harborview. Over the years, the manuscript developed in fits and starts with long periods when the muse deserted me altogether. Sheila Siden and Janice Van Cleve were among those who really helped me along in the early period. Others from the varied writers groups that Ariele hosted added critiques. I can see many of their faces but no longer remember names. Jere Smith, Garrit Hansen, and Roberta McKee from one of the last of Ariele's classes I attended gave valuable suggestions. Special thanks go to Ross McMeekin, writing instructor at Edmonds Community College, whose careful, in-depth reviews and suggestions, as well as the reviews by classmates April Ryan, Debbie Cooper, Stephanie O'Loughlin, and Cheryl Vezetinski led to improvements.

Thanks, too, to Sue Lechner, Harborview's engineering archivist, who took time from her busy day to share architect's floor plans from the original building—which solved the mystery of the wash basin in the admitting office. Nurses Nancy Radcliff and Helen Snortland helped me with details of partially remembered events. Dr. L.T. King, shared his early experiences as an intern and helped verify some of my own impressions. Kay Shirley, RHIA, clarified some details about the Medical Records Department and its procedures from that era. Dr. James McDermott corroborated details of the weekly psychiatric hearings from that time.

To Brittany Quon, my massage therapist, goes thanks for putting me in touch with her friend, Anna Katz, at Girl Friday Productions, who reviewed the manuscript in its entirety a year ago, and gave me over to Kristin Mehus-Roe, editor extraordinaire. She pushed me to re-organize and add data. My journal from long ago made it possible to put events into the proper time lines and flesh out details which brought the greater coherence she wanted to the narrative. Without Kristin's exemplary guidance, this would likely still be just a file on my computer. Thanks, too, to Laura Ware, cousin and retired copy-editor from the Santa Fe Institute, for her willingness to do a final edit of the manuscript before submission.

There are many people I worked with then whom I have not mentioned here but who are very much alive in my memory—Stephanie, Marge, Ellie and several Pattys. I hope they will forgive me.

ENDNOTES

In The Beginning

1   While researching building plans, I discovered the admitting office had been a full bathroom for the observation ward, with a connecting door. The only thing left was that wash basin.

A Necessary Annoyance

2   The basic elements that generally constituted a complete record were a history and physical, all orders and progress notes signed by the doctor who made them, a discharge summary, any consultation(s) done, and a dictated operative report on those patients who had surgery. Everything had to be signed by the doctor who was responsible. In the 1950s and 1960s, the history and physical and discharge summary were usually handwritten, as were the consultations, especially if done by a resident. Dictated reports were typed by medical transcriptionists in Medical Records, then added to the chart for the doctor to read over and sign. Signatures we got. Reading for accuracy? Not so much. Some things don't change.

3   One does have to wonder about the accuracy of an operative note or consultation done a month or more after the fact. Lawyers, too, have a field day raising such questions in malpractice claims. Checking the date of operation against the date of dictation was a common first step in reviewing subpoenaed medical records.

Lynn Regudon

Burn Treatment, Nature's Style

4   Thornton, D., Miles, B., Ralston, D. August, 2002. "Case Report: Maggot Therapy in an Acute Burn," *World Wide Wounds.*

Work And The Brilliant Peasants

5   A side note about disease and operation indexes: These were the beginning points for medical research. This task was begun by specially educated medical records professionals, coders who assigned numeric codes according to *The Standard Nomenclature of Diseases and Operations* (SNDO). The codes given to each diagnosis and operation (if there was one) were first entered on the patient record. Then each code from every chart was entered onto its appropriate five- by eight-inch card, one set holding the disease index, another the operations. Each entry required the patient's medical record number, code number(s) and discharge date. This manual-entry process was so redundant and labor-intensive, the job was almost always behind. The coding system changed in the 1960s to the *International Classification of Diseases* (ICD) which has undergone multiple revisions. The introduction of computers markedly reduced the labor-intensive nature of the process. Now, by entering the information once, one can retrieve vast amounts of data, currently used for both research and billing.

From Flintstones to Jetsons

6   Devereux, Greg, "Opinion: Guest: UW has strayed from Harborview's public mission" *Seattle Times,* August 10, 2014.

7   Claridge, Christine, "UW, King County reach agreement on running Harborview Medical Center," *Seattle Times*, February 1, 2016.

Some Thoughts About The Future

8   *Deadly Delivery:The Maternal Health Care Crisis in the US,* Amnesty International, p. 1.

9   Hussey PS, Anderson GF, Osborn R, et al. (2004). "How does the quality of care compare in five countries?" *Health affairs (Project Hope)* **23** (3): 89–99.

10   "Progress Report on Cancer Control in Canada." *Centre for Chronic Disease Prevention and Control*, 2004 pg. 11.

11   *Seattle Times*, September 26, 2014.

12   Jauhar, Sandeep, *Doctored: The Disillusionment of an American Doctor*, Farrar, Strauss and Giroux, New York, 2014, p. 97, 98.

13   Belk, David, MD, *Huffington Post*, blog, "It ain't the Lawyers: Medical Malpractice Costs have been Dropping." Updated 1/23/14. Specialists are hardest hit here, too, with orthopedic surgeons paying approximately $20,000, as opposed to internists' and family practice costs of around $3,000 per year. Costs also vary around the country.

14   Physicians involved in this model of care accept far fewer patients, only those who pay a retainer fee, with or without insurance coverage. The doctors are available for same day or next day appointments, able to spend longer times with each patient. These are primary care doctors who manage each patient's care and develop closer relationships. One issue is that this takes yet another physician away from the general patient population. Lab and minor procedures are billed separately, usually on a cash basis over and above the retainer fee. Hospitalizations and referrals to outside specialists would not be covered either.

15   Jauhar, Sandeep, *Doctored: The Disillusionment of the American Physician*, Farrar, Strauss and Giroux, New York, 2014, p. 106.

16   Young, Audrey, MD, *The House of Hope and Fear*, Sasquatch Books, Seattle, WA, 2009, p 231.

17   Kaplan, Esther, "American Speedup," *The Nation* 20, November 17, 2014, 29-33.

Lightning Source UK Ltd.
Milton Keynes UK
UKOW02f1124270217
295415UK00002B/643/P